Excel 2024

For Beginners

I0446266

A Step-by-Step Approach to Mastering
Fundamental Formula, Function and Chart
with Simple and Real-Life Examples.

James Stunner

Table of Content

Introduction

Microsoft Excel is a popular and frequently used spreadsheet tool developed by Microsoft as part of the Microsoft Office productivity software package. It is primarily intended for data management, analysis, and visualization operations. It features a spreadsheet application that provides a grid of cells organized into rows and columns to create a worksheet. Within these cells, users can enter, save, and modify data. Users can input various data types into Excel cells, such as numbers, text, dates, and formulas.

Excel allows users to perform calculations on data using formulas and functions. Formulas are custom expressions that utilize cell references and operators, while functions are predefined operations, such as SUM, AVERAGE, or IF, that simplify common calculations. It offers numerous tools for data analysis, including sorting, filtering, and creating charts and graphs to visualize and interpret data. Users can structure data by creating multiple worksheets within a workbook, making managing and organising related information easier.

Excel features PivotTables, a powerful tool for summarizing and analyzing large datasets. It enables users to create dynamic reports and gain insights from complex data. It provides data validation rules to ensure the accuracy and consistency of data input into cells.

In Excel, users can apply formatting to cells based on specific conditions, making it easier to identify trends or anomalies in the data. It supports data importation from various sources, such as databases and external files, and exporting data in different formats, including CSV, PDF, and more.

Multiple users can collaborate on the same Excel workbook simultaneously, allowing for collaborative data analysis and sharing. Users can automate repetitive tasks by recording and running macros, which are sequences of actions. Excel offers security features to protect workbooks with passwords and control access to sensitive information.

Excel is used for various applications, including financial modelling, budgeting, data tracking, project management, and reporting. It is a versatile tool used in various industries, from finance and accounting to marketing and research, for tasks involving structured data.

Chapter One

Microsoft Excel

Microsoft Excel is a universal computer software program designed by Microsoft that organizes, manipulates, analyses, and stores data (particularly numerical data) arranged in rows and columns. This computer program is primarily a spreadsheet application with vast features. It possesses the basic features of all spreadsheet applications coupled with other statistical, engineering, financial graphing, and programming functions. Microsoft Excel is one of the Microsoft Office and Office 365 suite of software, and it can interact with Microsoft applications in the Office Suite.

It was designed for use with operating systems such as Windows, Android, and Apple OS. Microsoft Excel (or MS Excel) has been in use since its initial release in 1985 (about 38 years ago), and the program has evolved over the years, increasing its features and functions. In

1985, Microsoft launched MS Excel as "MS Multiplan," and it began to compete with similar spreadsheet applications. Lotus 1-2-3 of Lotus Development Corp. was one of them. Multiplan had a graphical user interface, making inputting and manipulating data in spreadsheets easier and faster. However, it was built only for Apple Inc.'s Macintosh computer, restricting its use to Macintosh users.

In 1987, Microsoft released an updated version compatible with its new Microsoft Windows operating system, making MS Excel more versatile. Following this, updated versions with new significant elements such as 3-D charts, outlining abilities, toolbars, auto-fill functions, shortcuts, and more automated functions were released. In 1995, Microsoft changed the program's name to Microsoft Excel to tell the year of its main release. New updates were released in the following years until 2007, when version 12 was released. This version switched to using the more open and organized XLXS files. In 2019, the most current version, 16, with exceptional features, was launched and is now used in many businesses worldwide for financial analysis. Although Microsoft does not release new versions of MS Excel, new features and improvements are brought on automatically over time.

There are numerous benefits of using MS Excel. Excel is beneficial to individuals both personally and professionally. Hardly any profession does not require the functions MS Excel provides for data presentation, analysis, and storage. Excel allows for the efficient storage and management of any size of data, ranging from small data sets to larger ones, such as a list of employees' information, employees' payroll, revenues, and product inventories of large businesses and institutions. It also makes it easier to trace, access, and even filter these data at any time. Excel consists of simple to complex functions and formulas (like SUM and AVERAGE) that enable arithmetic calculations and manipulations of data in less time. 3-D bar charts, pie charts, line graphs, and other graphical tools allow Excel to analyze and present data in more detail. One of the most prominent uses of Excel is to increase efficiency. This increased work efficiency makes an individual more relevant in the workplace, positioning one for career promotions. Also, knowledge of Excel opens doors to better career opportunities because businesses use the application for different processes like projects, data, accounts, and human resource management.

Regardless of one's ultimate career goals, Excel is an essential and impressive skill to acquire. The numerous features, formulas, and functions may be simple or complex. It can carry out simple arithmetic such as addition, subtraction, division, and multiplication. The autofill feature is also a common element of the application. To get the sum of values in cells A2 to A6, click on the cell you want to result in and type the formula "=A2+A3+A4+A5+A6".

Chapter Two

Excel Download

The MS Excel application can be installed on a desktop or mobile phone. The guide to downloading the application depends on the type of device the application you're downloading the application on. Excel is a part of the Microsoft Office software applications and thus can be used on a desktop with this software package installed. Computer manufacturers (such as Dell, HP, and Acer) may install Microsoft Office packages already with the Windows operating system of the computer installed on the computer. Windows 11 is said to be integrated with the Microsoft Office package.

However, in the absence of the Microsoft Office package on a computer, the software package is downloaded from the Microsoft official website on the Internet. Once the Microsoft software package is installed on the computer, MS Excel is invariably installed. Macbooks with macOS also require the Microsoft Office package to be downloaded and installed on the computer to have the Excel application. To download the Office package from the Internet, one must buy a subscription to access Microsoft Office 365 products. Once the subscription plan is bought, there is access to download Microsoft Office. There is also the option to download a free trial of Microsoft Office for one month, but one will have to provide a means of payment before the download. At the end of the trial, an individual account is automatically billed for using Microsoft Office. It is important to note that without a Microsoft account, one cannot buy a subscription to Microsoft Office 365. Therefore, at the point of download, one has to create a new account (if unavailable) and log into their Microsoft account. Upon successful login into one's Microsoft account and buying a Microsoft Office 365 plan, select the "install" icon and select the correct product (Microsoft Office/Microsoft Office 365 in this case) you want to install. Also, select a destination for the downloading file. Finally, the file is set up after downloading, and installation is completed. It involves steps that vary depending on the operating system. You can then search for Excel in the software package downloaded. You can also download Microsoft Office free on a desktop using Microsoft reward gift cards on the website, but acquiring rewards will take some time to afford you to buy Microsoft Office. Members of staff or students enrolled in educational institutions with special contracts and partnerships with Microsoft have the privilege to download Microsoft without payment using the school's Microsoft account.

On the other hand, Excel can be downloaded for free directly on a mobile phone (Android or iOS). You don't have to buy a subscription or download the Office software package to use Excel on a mobile phone. The application is downloaded from the "App Store" and "Play Store" on iOS and Android phones. Once the application is downloaded and installed on the phone, you can open the application. However, you must log into your Microsoft account before you can begin use. Excel's unlimited technical resources and skills, especially for businesses and organizations, cannot be overemphasized. Excel is useful for efficient analysis of complex financial reports, efficient management of projects, and human resources of a company. Allowing you to be on track with every aspect of the organization. All these gather reasons why the application should be used even if it comes at a price. The benefits it offers are worth its cost.

Excel Extensions

Excel files are saved in different formats or extensions. Because MS Excel has undergone many upgrades, there have also been upgrades in the file extensions. Among the numerous extensions of Excel files that we have, the popular ones used after the 2007 MS Excel upgrade include ".xlsx," ".xlsm," ".xlsb," ".xltx," ".xltm." ".xls" was the default Excel file extension before the 2007 Excel version. An extension is used depending on the type and elements of the Excel file. It also tells the active sheet of the file.

For example, ".xlsx" is the default and most common extension of Excel files since the 2007 upgrade, and it is mostly used when the worksheet or workbook is the active cell. However, it cannot be used to save Microsoft Visual Basic for Applications macro code or Excel macro sheets. Rather, ".xlsm" saves those Excel files with programming languages. ".xlsb" is the extension used for Excel Binary Workbook files. Extensions are located in the "Save As Type" dialogue box. When you want to save an Excel file on your device, and you click the "Save As" option (which is located in the "File" menu), Excel automatically gives an extension compatible with the file in the "Save As type." Nevertheless, you can also view the list of Excel extensions and select your choice, which must be compatible with the file's content.

Chapter Three

Excel Interface

Excel is a perfect tool to analyze and get insights from your data, but it has many menus and buttons. We will review them so you can understand your data's story. Let's start with how you can even get Excel.

There are two different ways to get started with Excel. The first way is to navigate to www.excel.new in your web browser. You'll need to log in, and that's entirely free. It drops you into a brand-new spreadsheet directly in your web browser.

Excel on the web has most of the functionality in the desktop app; typically, new features hit the web first. Secondly, you can install Excel on your desktop, but you must purchase Microsoft 365. When you launch Excel for the first time, you'll land on the start page. You can jump into a blank new workbook in the top left-hand corner.

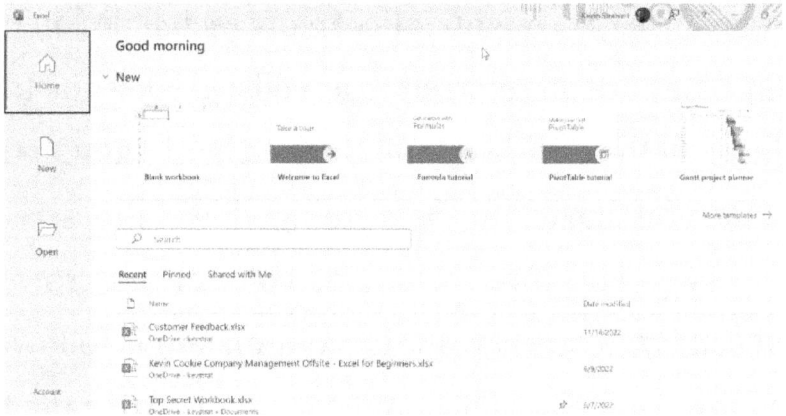

On the right, you have a whole host of templates. It's worth looking through them to see if one meets your needs. Below, you can return to your recent workbooks; on the top, you can search for a workbook. In the top left-hand corner, click into a blank, which drops you into a brand-new workbook.

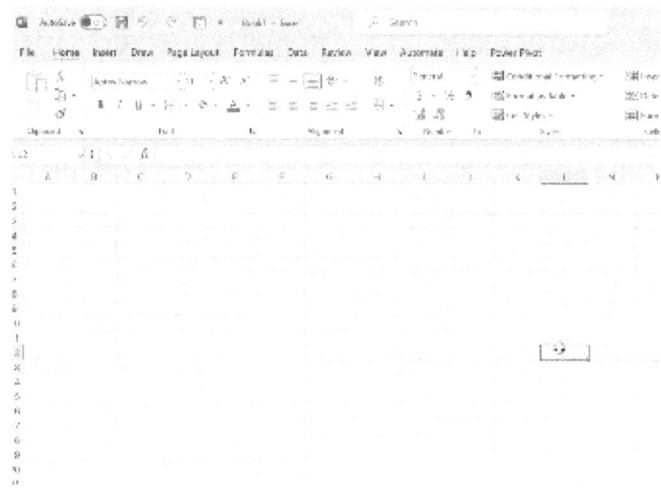

At first glance, you might notice many rectangles on the screen. They are all referred to as cells. Across the top, you have all the different letters called columns. On the left side, you have numbers going down the screen called rows. The intersection of column and row is called cell E7. It starts with the column and is followed by the row. In the top left-hand corner, you have the E7 in the name box and can change the name.

To make things easier, you can zoom in and out. In the bottom right-hand corner, you can zoom in or out. You can also press control and then move your mouse wheel up or down, which will zoom in and out.

Excel Interface and Tabs

The Excel interface can be categorized into five important sections: the title bar, the ribbon, the formula bar, the worksheet area, and the status bar. The title bar houses the "quick access toolbar," where you can store favourite and most frequently used icons, the file (or workbook) name, which is usually followed by the application name (Excel), and the Windows control buttons – the minimize, maximize and close buttons.

In Microsoft 365, Excel shows the profile of the account user in the header. The ribbon (formerly known as the toolbar) consists of tabs and commands that allow you to maximize the application features. The ribbon consists of nine tabs – "Home," "Insert," "Formulas," "Page Layout," "Data," "Review," "View," "Developer," "Add-ins," and Script Lab." The file menu is also present in the ribbon. The tabs are made up of commands, which are categorized based on the singular tasks they perform. These tasks are also summarized into groups such as the "Sort & Filter" under the "data" tab.

The Home tab is the default tab that shows when Excel is opened. Some groups have launch buttons that take you to dialogue boxes with more commands. There are also contextual tabs that only reveal themselves when an object on the worksheet is selected. For example, the "table design" chart only appears when a table in the worksheet is selected. The formula bar, which is below the ribbon, is where formulas can be typed and edited.

To the left side of the formula bar, the name or address box, which tells the name of the selected cell, is seen. This selected cell is active; a coloured rectangular box usually surrounds its borders. A cell is the point where the lettered column and numbered row meet. Hence, the name of a cell has the letter of the column and the number of the row in which it is located, and It is the smallest functional unit of a spreadsheet where data is entered.

The next section is the worksheet. The worksheet is made up of numerous cells in rows and columns. Rows are a horizontally arranged data entry, while columns are a vertically arranged data entry. Numbers identify rows, while columns are identified by letters. Rows and columns are about 1,048,076 and 16, 384 respectively, making over 17 billion cells in one worksheet.

A workbook (a collection of worksheets) can contain multiple worksheets. The worksheets in a workbook are in the worksheet tab below the worksheet area. A new worksheet can be added to a workbook by clicking the plus sign at the worksheet tab. By default, "Sheet1" or "Sheet2" is seen depending on the number of the sheet, but this worksheet can be renamed.

The worksheet has a vertical and horizontal scroll bar that allows you to navigate the cells of the worksheet area. The horizontal scroll bar is located in the worksheet tab. Finally, the status bar is a thin bar at the end of the Excel interface that contains different page view layouts of the worksheet and the zoom control of the worksheet area. The figure below shows a labelled general overall layout of the Excel interface.

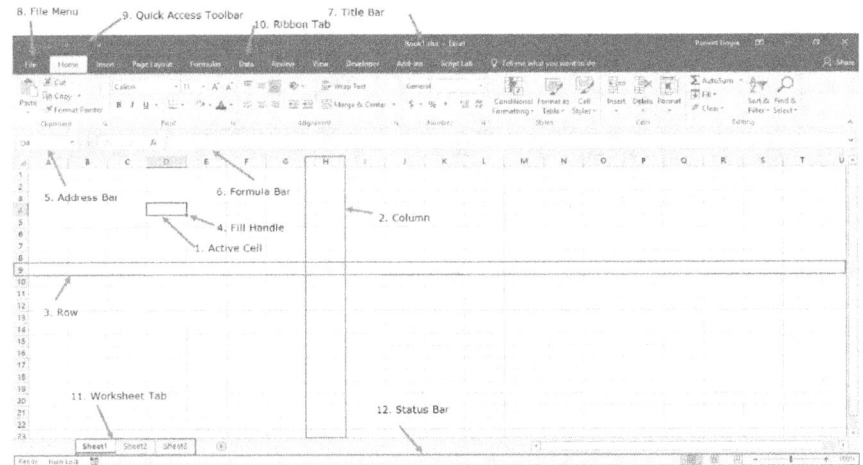

Excel Formulas and Functions

Excel formulas allow one to perform arithmetic operations such as addition, multiplication, subtraction, and division on numerical values in a set of cells. When typed correctly, these formulas always give a result, even if it is a mistake by the user. Excel

15

functions are inbuilt predefined expressions in Excel that are also used to perform mathematical calculations and other specific functions on different data types. They are similar to Excel formulas and are mostly used interchangeably. Excel functions have names that tell the operational use.

These names are used rather than the conventional mathematical operators. Numerous Excel formulas and functions perform different operations on different data types, such as numbers, word characters, dates, and time. Excel formulas and functions reduce the labour and time used in mathematical calculations and other functions. Excel formulas are only used for arithmetic operations of numerical data because only the operators can be used.

Meanwhile, Excel functions are used for tasks on numbers and other data type. The basic Excel functions necessary for beginners to be acquainted with include the "SUM," "IF," COUNT," "COUNTA," "AVERAGE," "MIN and "MAX," "TIME," "DATE," "POWER," "CEILING" and "FLOOR" functions. The "SUM" function is the most basic and primary function to be known. As the name implies, it adds up the numbers in two or more cells.

The "COUNT" function counts the number of cells with numerical values in a selected range of cells, while the "COUNTA" function counts all types of data (including numbers) in a selected range of cells. MIN and MAX show the minimum and maximum values in a range of cells, respectively. Functions such as DATE, TIME, and TRIM are non-mathematical functions of Excel. DATE functions like NOW or TODAY tell the current day and time.

The TRIM function eliminates empty spaces within a function or formula, so Excel does not view them as errors. It is like a function within a function; it only operates on a single cell, not a range of cells like other functions. The list of Excel formulas and functions goes on and is almost inexhaustible.

To operate, choose the cell you for the result and then begin to input the formula by typing the equal sign "=." It is followed by entering the name of the first cell with the data to be operated on. Add an operator like the +,

-, *, and / signs, followed by the name of the cell with the next data value. The number of cell addresses/names in the formula depends on the intended operation. Once the formula for the operation is completed, press the "Enter" button on the keyboard to produce a result in the cell. Excel functions also start with the equal sign, but unlike formulas, this is followed by the function name, the name of the cell with the first data you intend to calculate, the column sign (:), and the name of the cell with the last number. For example, the Excel formula to multiply data values in cells in A2 and B3 would be "=A2*B3" (figure 2), while the Excel function would be "=PRODUCTA2:A3" (figure 3). The formula used in the cell should be seen in the formula bar. Formulas can also be edited in the formula bar.

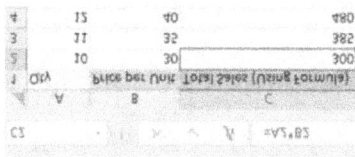

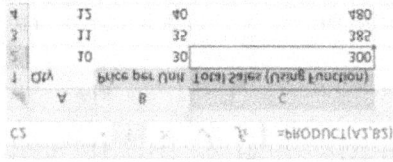

Chapter Four

Excel for Beginners

Certain processes make the use of Excel more efficient and effective. New users of the application can acquaint themselves with such processes. They include:

Customizing the Quick Access Toolbar

Instead of hunting through the ribbons for frequently used commands, users can add these commands to the Quick Access Toolbar (QAT, as it is fondly called) for quick access. The QAT is located at the foremost left side of the title bar. The simplest way to add a command to the QAT would be to right-click on the command you want to add to the QAT and then select the "Add to Quick Access Toolbar" that appears on the shortcut that appears.

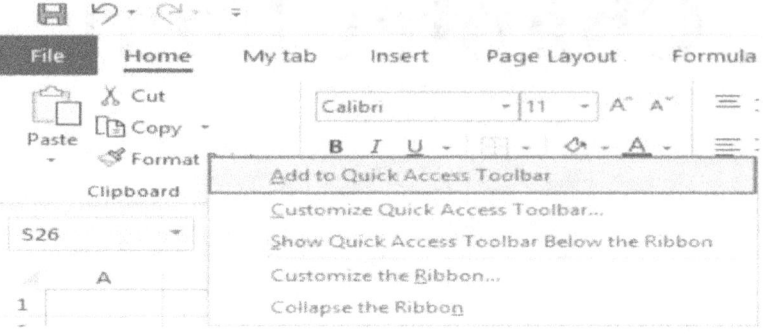

Also, you could click on the drop-down arrow located at the far right of QAT. A series of commands will be seen in the shortcut menu that appears.

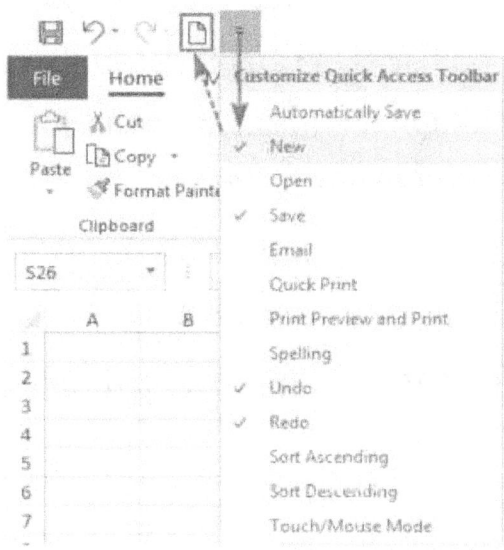

Select the command of choice, and it immediately adds to the QAT. If the command of choice is not seen on the shortcut menu, you can select the "More Commands" option.

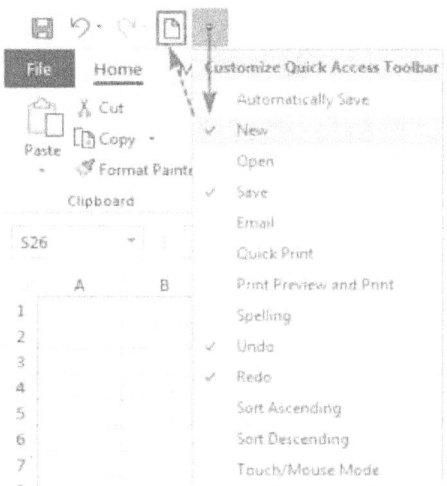

A menu list of **"Excel Option">** **"Quick Access Toolbar"** that allows you to customize the QAT appears. The list on the left tab contains all commands, while the commands already in QAT are on the right list. Click on the command of choice on the left side, and select the "Add" icon between the two sides. The command goes to the right list. Press "OK" to activate the change.

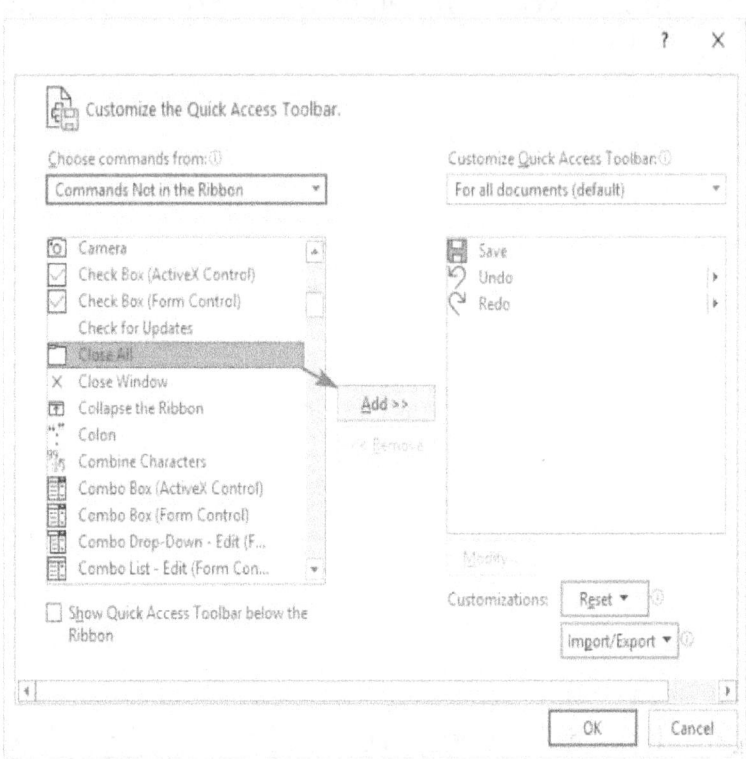

Data Filtering

Data filtering allows you to organize data in various cells or tables. When you filter a data set, data not within the filter criteria is hidden, leaving only data within the criteria. This allows one to focus on the set of data chosen. To filter data in a range of cells, you select any cell within the range of cells to be filtered. Then select the Filter command under the Data tab.

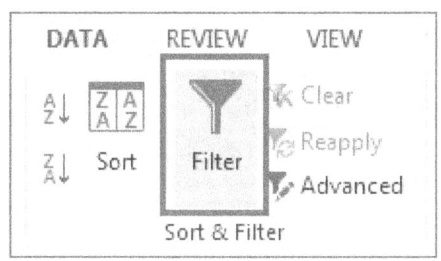

Click on the header column ▼ that at the first cell in the column. Select Text Filter or Number Filter (depending on the data type). Select any of the Excel data filter prompts (such as "Between..." or "Greater than...") seen in the shortcut menu that appears.

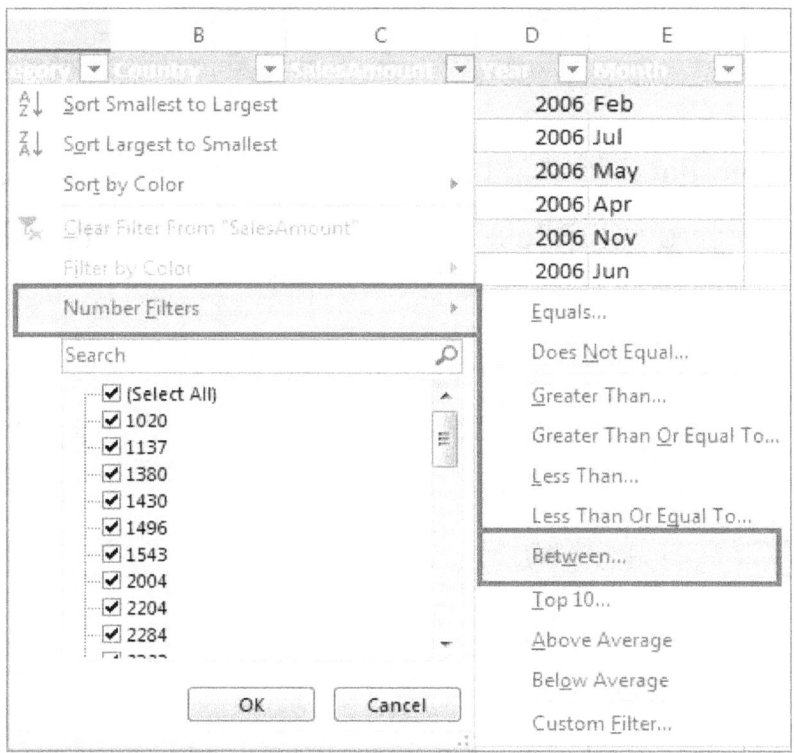

Complete the filter criteria to suit your choice. Click "OK" to confirm the action.

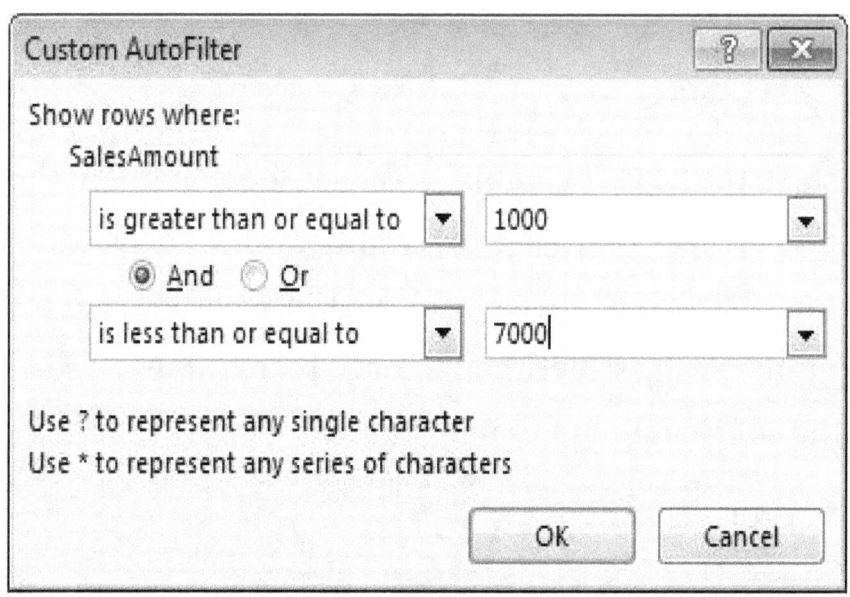

To filter data in a table, one can select the header column arrow for the column that needs to be filtered.

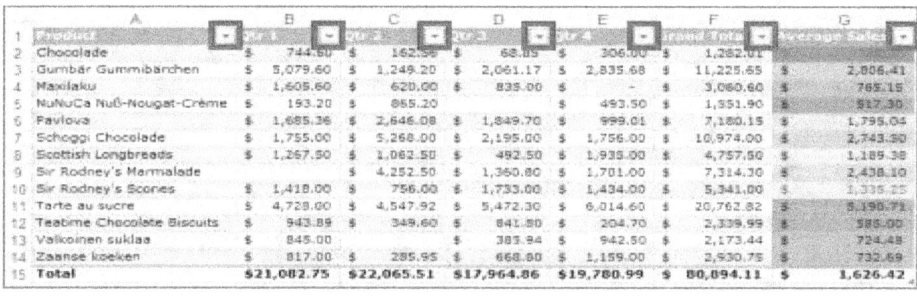

Uncheck the "Select All" option and the boxes you do not want to show. Click "OK" to confirm the action.

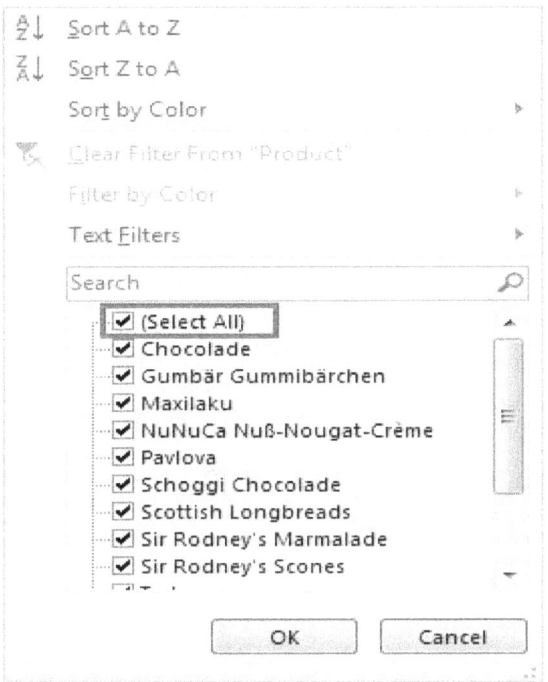

After filtering, the header column changes to a filter icon which allows you to undo filtering.

Incorporating Dynamic Headers and Footers

For better presentation and readability of an Excel file, headers and footers can be added to a workbook. This action divides the worksheet into printable pages, enhancing the file's organisation. Headers and footers in Excel can contain different information. They could include basic information such as the workbook name, date, and page numbers or customized information like specific texts, logos, and other images. This information also improves the professional aesthetics of the file. Also, different headers and footers can be used on different pages. Special codes, functions, and a combination of texts must incorporate dynamic headers and footers. To insert a header and footer in Excel, go to the "Text" group in the "Insert" tab and click the "Header & Footer" command. This will turn the worksheet into a Page Layout view with a header and footer.

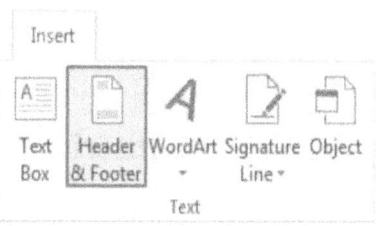

Now, you can customize the header or footer and put any information you choose. If you want the header on the page's right, left, or centre, click the corresponding side and enter the information. Ditto for the footer. Click any other area of the worksheet to save changes and exit the area. Press Esc on the header or footer box to remove changes. You can enter header and footer elements such as file name and page number by selecting the "Design" tab in the header or footer box and selecting any preferred element from the "Header & Footer" group.

The figure below shows the entering of the page number to the right side of the footer. The "Navigation" group allows you to select the commands displayed in the "Header & Footer group. You can also add Excel inbuilt header and footer elements (preset headers and footers). Do this by going to the header or footer box and selecting the "Design" tab. Then, choose any preset element by selecting either the "Header' or "Footer" icon in the "Header & Footer" group. The figure below also shows the insertion of a preset footer element of page number and file name. However, when using the preset elements, the side of the displayed footer or header is also inbuilt (or preset). A user cannot change this.

Also, most preset Excel header and footer elements can be entered as special codes. For example, the "&[Page]" and "&[File]" are codes for page number and file name, respectively. You can click the footer or header with these elements to view these codes. Just like Excel formulas, typing these codes manually into the footer or header box will also give its corresponding element.

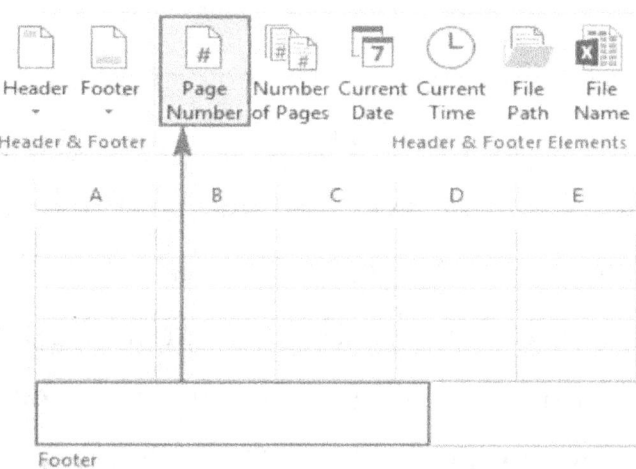

Figure showing entering of the page number to the right side of the footer

1   2

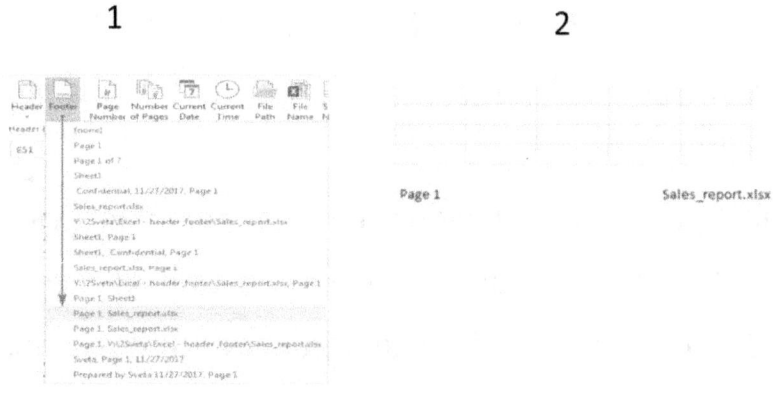

Figures showing the choice of preset footer element and the display outcome.

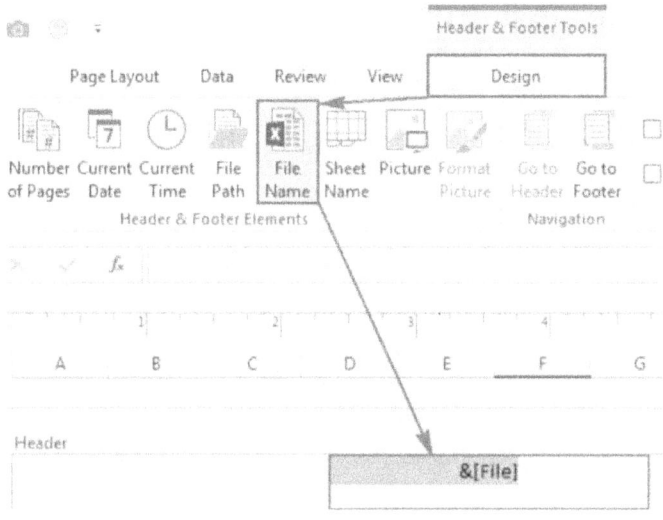

Figure showing code of header element – file name.

Defining Print Regions

A print region consists of one or more cells selected to be printed when the whole worksheet is not printed. Only the print region is printed when you print a worksheet after defining the print region. A worksheet can contain more than one print region. To define a printing area, select the cells that you want to designate as a printing area. Then select the "Page Setup" group in the 'Page Layout" tab, and then click the "Print Area" command. Click the "Set Print Area" icon. To add more cells to the already defined print region, select the cells to be added and then select the "Add to Print Area" icon in the "Print Area" command. The print area is saved when the workbook is saved.

1   2

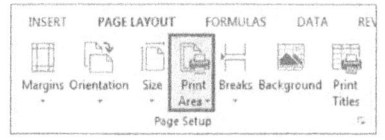 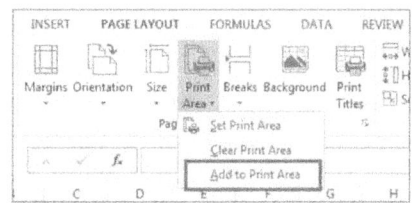

Paste Special Options

When you copy and paste in Excel, all cell contents – data, formula, formatting, and comments- are copied and pasted into the new cell. However, the "Paste Special" option allows you to select the element of the cell you want to paste. Select the cell or cells you want to paste data to do this. Click the "Home" tab, followed by the "Paste" command, and then the "Paste Special" icon.

The Paste Special box, which contains all special options to be pasted, is seen (see figure below). Pick the special option and press "OK" to confirm the selection. The keyboard shortcut "Ctrl+Alt+V" can also reveal Paste Special options.

1

2

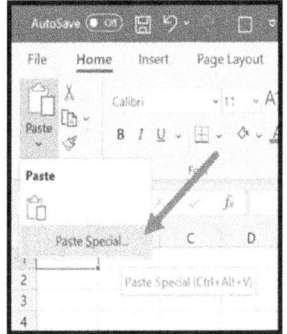 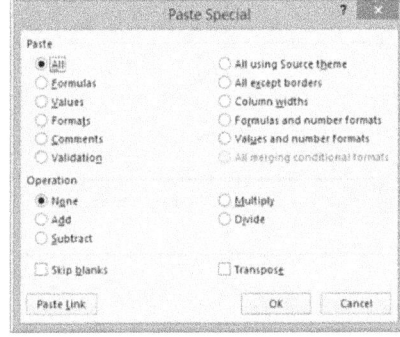

Grouping and Ungrouping Columns To Hide Detailed Data

Sometimes, organising a worksheet with plenty of columns may be handy. Columns are organized into groups that can be shown or hidden. To group columns, select all cells in the column or columns that want to be grouped. In the "Data tab," select the "Outline" group and then click the "Group" command. The group is immediately created, and the outline symbol is displayed at the top of the worksheet. Click the "square minus" symbol to "collapse" and hide grouped columns. The "square plus" expands and shows the grouped columns. Go to "Data > Outline," select "Ungroup," and then click "Clear Outline" to ungroup columns.

1   2   3

Keeping Papers and Workbooks Safe

There are levels to keeping an Excel file safe. One can prevent unauthorized access and editing to the worksheet area, the workbook structure (between the worksheets), and the Excel file. To keep others from disturbing the structure of a workbook, Click "Review > Protect Workbook" and check the "Structure." If you want a password, enter a password in the Password box. Click "OK" and enter the password again to confirm it. Select "OK" again to complete the process.

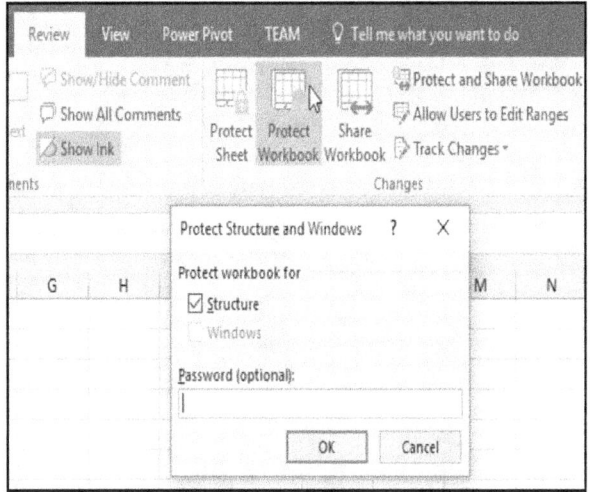

To protect the worksheet area, select "Review > Protect Worksheet." In the "Protect Sheet" box, you can select elements you want others to be able to change in the "Allow all users of this worksheet to" list (see figure below). You can also set an optional password.

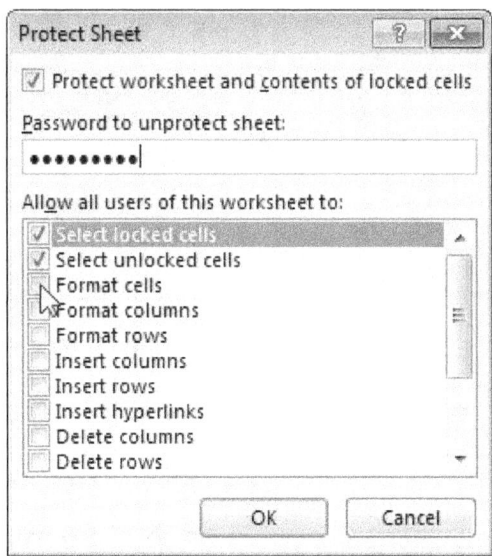

To prevent others from even opening the Excel file, follow these sequential pictorial steps:

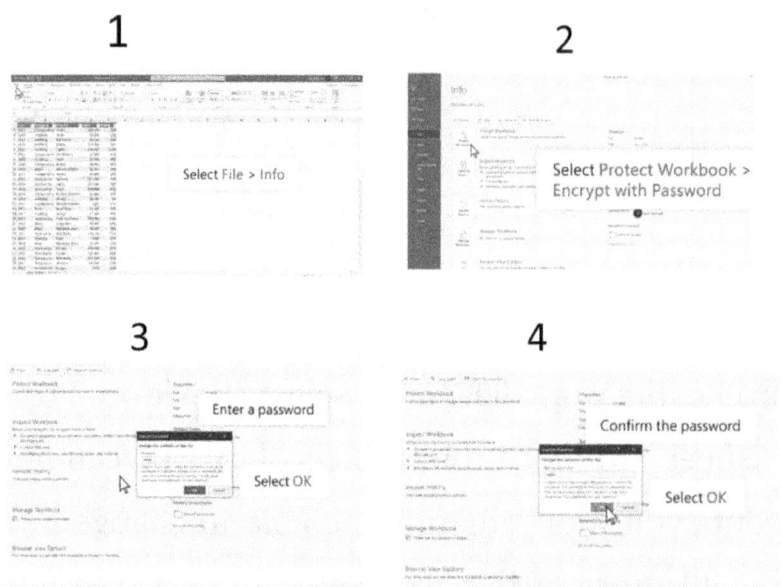

Caution: ensure the chosen password is memorable, as Excel cannot remember the forgotten password, and without this password, the file cannot be opened.

Finding Precedents and Dependent Formulations
Precedence and dependence relationship between cells and formulas can be traced in excel by clicking the "Trace Precedents" or "Trace Dependents" command in the "Formula auditing" group of the "Formulas" tab in the cell you want to trace the precedent or dependent

for. The precedent tool shows the cells involved in a formula using arrows, while the dependent tool shows the cells dependent on the selected cells with arrows. If there are multiple precedents or dependents, you can use the "Trace precedents" or "Trace Dependents" tools again to trace the precedents of precedent cells or dependents of dependent cells.

E3		fx	=C3 * D3	
	A	B	C	D	E
1					
2		Product	Qty	Unit Price	Total Price 2019
3		Almonds	2	7.5	15
4		Coffee	1	34.5	34.5
5		Chocolate	5	9.56	47.8

Figure showing precedent cells of cell E3

	A	B	C	D	E
1					
2		Product	Qty	Unit Price	Total Price 2019
3		Almonds	2	7.5	15
4		Coffee	1	34.5	34.5
5		Chocolate	5	9.56	47.8

Figure showing dependent cells of cell D3

Validation of Data In The Cell Drop-Down Menu

Data validation is used in Excel to specify the data that can be entered into a cell or a range of cells. A drop-down list can be created to tell the data to be validated in these cells. Begin by making entries into cells of the worksheet to create the drop-down list. An example is shown in images.

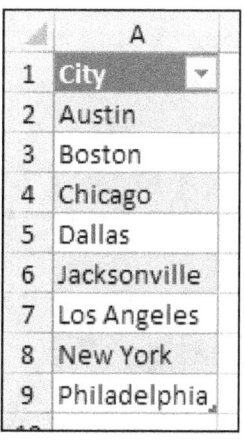

Select the cells in the worksheet in which you want to validate the drop-down list. Go to "Data > Data Validation" in the ribbon. Select "list" in the "Allow" box of the "Settings" tab. Check the "Ignore blank" box to see if any cell can remain empty. Check the "In-cell drop-down" box. Type the source of the drop-down list in the "Source" box.

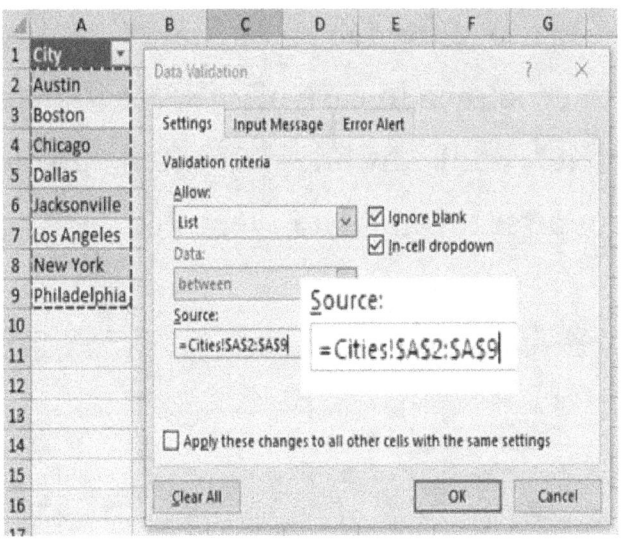

Move to the "Input Message" and check the "Show input message when cell is selected" box if you want this option. Type the title and the input message you want to be seen in the corresponding boxes. Uncheck the box if you do not want any messages seen.

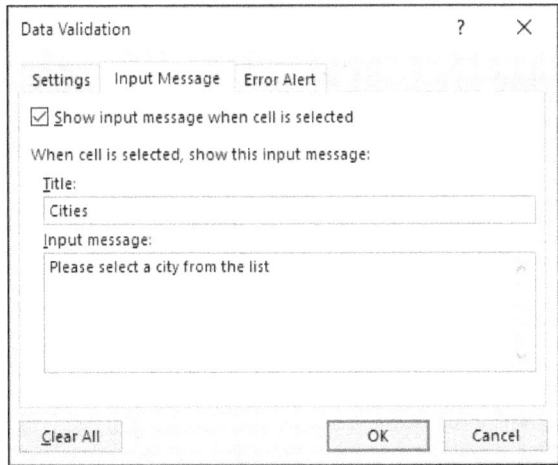

Select the "Error Alert" tab to set the title and style of the error to be shown in case of an error in data input. If you do not want any message seen, uncheck the "Show error after invalid data is entered" box.

Creating Simple Graphs

Graphs (charts) are very useful for visualising data, and Excel provides many graphs that can be used. Creating simple popular graphs like bar charts, pie charts, line graphs, etc. involves the following steps.

Firstly, select the data for which you want to create a graph.

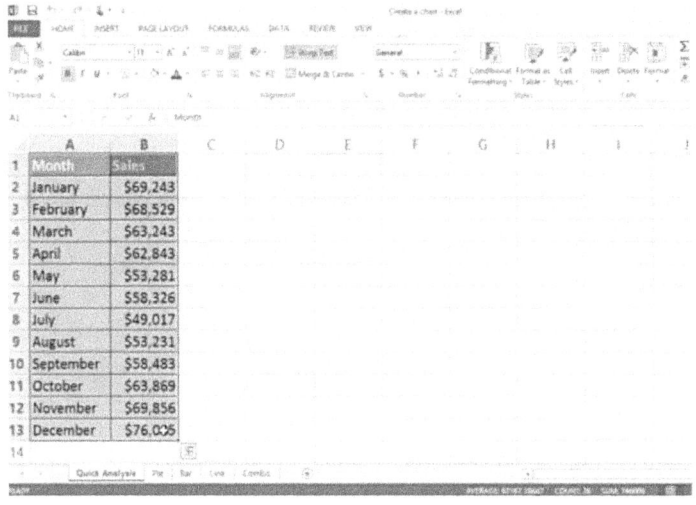

Click the "Quick Analysis" icon below the cells, and select the 'Charts" tab. Or click the "Insert > Recommended Charts" tab in the ribbon. Excel lists recommended charts for the selected data in both cases. If the preferred chart is not displayed, select the "All Charts" icon in the "Insert" tab or "other charts" in the "Quick Analysis" chart tab and select your preferred chart. Click "OK".

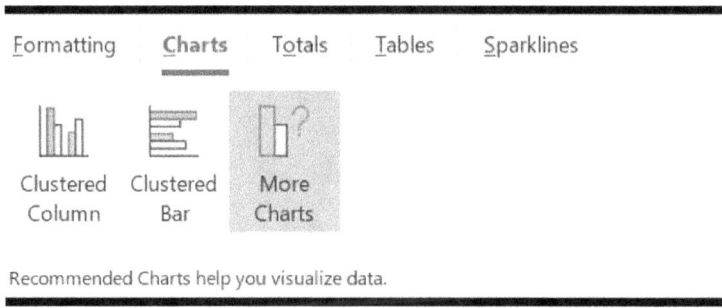

Figure showing Quick Analysis Tool > Charts > More Charts

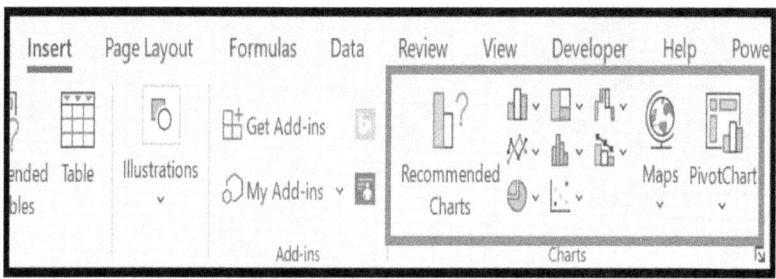

Figure showing "Insert > Charts"

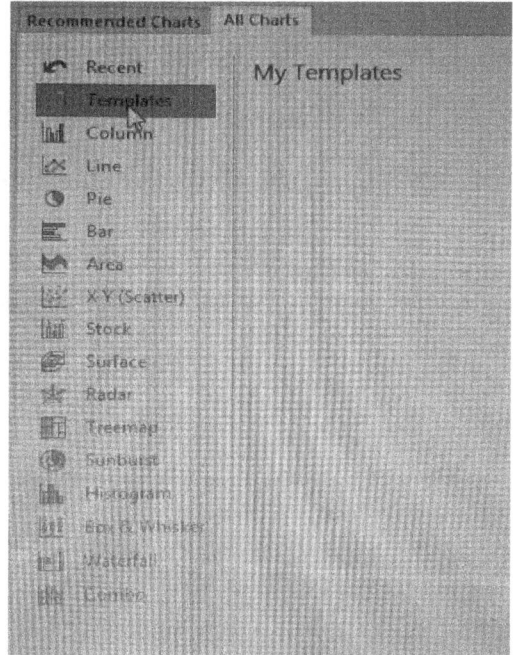

Figure showing "Insert > Charts > Recommended Charts >All Charts"

You can use "Chart Elements," "Chart Styles," and "Chart Filter" in the upper right corner of the chart to add chart elements such as axes labels, legends, data labels, etc. you can also find other editing options I the "Design and "Format" tabs in the ribbon.

Chart Design   Format

Chapter Five

Excel For Medium-Level Users

Other sophisticated and "complex" Excel functions are common among older and more frequent application users. They may be intermediate or advanced-level functions.

Intermediate Skills

A brief list of intermediate Excel skills would include excellent use of visual data presentation features such as Excel tables, graphs and charts, Pivot tables, sparklines, etc, and good knowledge of data manipulating, formatting, and filtering skills that save time and increase efficiency. These data management skills may include the use of Excel features like the "Go to special," range names, "Quick Analysis Tool," "Data validation," "Paste Special," and text-to-columns. The "Go to special" option takes one to certain types of cells, like blank cells or cells with formulas. To get to this icon, go to Home Tab → Editing → Find and Select → Go To special (Figure 1). The "Go to special" box shows, select the type of cells you want to find, e.g. blank cells

1

2

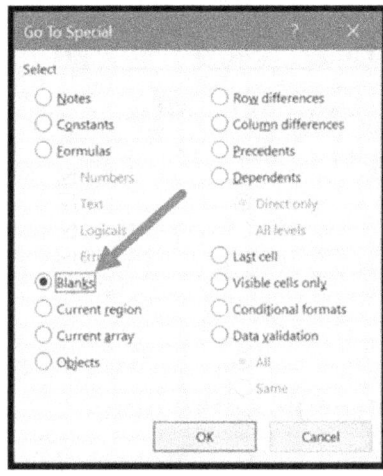

Range names involve giving a cell or range of cells a new name or address. To do this, go to Formula Tab → Define Names → Define name. Fill in the new name dialogue box as seen below.

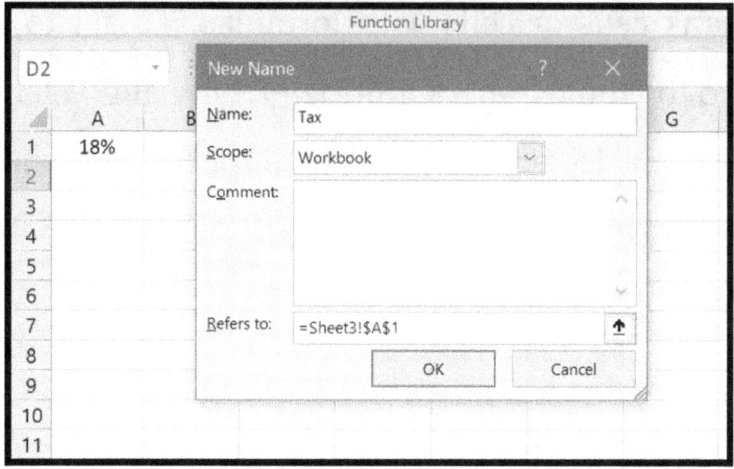

Cells or cells are referred to by that name, even when writing formulas like in the figure below.

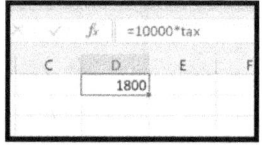

Text-to-columns allow you to make multiple columns within a single column to understand data better. With the Quick Analysis Tool, you can quickly access regular commands in the ribbon, such as chart formatting. The arrow in the figure points to the Quick Analysis Tool

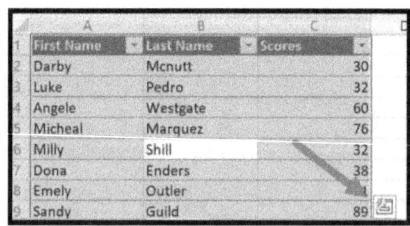

Using logical functions such as COUNTIF, SUMIF, SUBTOTAL, and XLOOKUP also improves efficiency. At the intermediate level, a user should be able to create macro codes for Visual Basic for Application programming language.

Excel Keyboard Shortcut

The Excel Keyboard shortcuts are numerous, just like its functions, and one can barely exhaust knowing them all. Basic and frequently used shortcuts include "Ctrl+O" (to the new workbook) and "Ctrl+W" (to close a workbook). Ctrl+9 is used to hide selected rows, while Ctrl+0 hides selected columns. Alt+H, D, and C delete a column. In Excel, once the Alt key is pressed, the ribbon shortcuts, known as key tips, are displayed in the the ribbon (see key tips in figure). Combination of Alt and key tips for Access keys such as Alt+H, Alt+N, Alt+P, Alt+A, Alt+W, and Alt+M that are shortcuts to the Home, Insert, Page Layout, Data, View, and Formulas tabs, respectively. You can also work within the ribbon with keyboard shortcuts, such as the arrow keys to move among tabs and items or Ctrl+F1 to expand and collapse the ribbon.

There are also keys to move along the cells, such as Shift+Tab, which is used to move to the previous cell that was worked on in a worksheet, and Ctrl+Home to home to the beginning of a worksheet. The arrow keys are useful to move along the cells in the corresponding direction. There also exists keyboard shortcuts to format cells, e.g., "Ctrl+Shift+Number sign (#)" to apply date format, and "Ctrl+Shift+At sign (@)" to apply time format to a cell. Ctrl+D allows you to fill down the contents or format of the first cell into the adjacent cells in a selected range of cells. The Paste Special dialog box appears after pressing "Ctrl+Alt+V or "Alt+E+S." To select an option in the dialogue box, press the letter underlined in the option of choice. There are many keyboard shortcuts to select cells and perform actions. Some shortcuts are specific for dates, formula bars, and functions. The F function keys are also not left out. Some Microsoft Word shortcuts, such as Ctrl+C, Ctrl+B, Ctrl+V, Ctrl+S, Ctrl+Z, and Ctrl+S, perform the same functions.

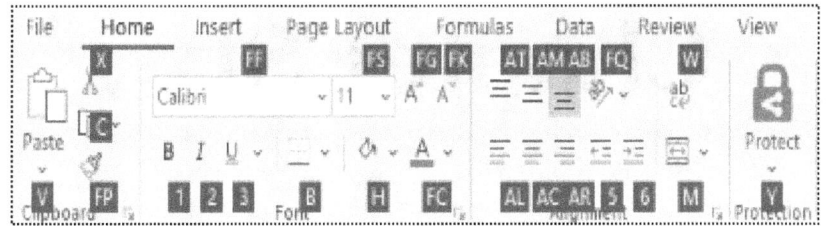

Ribbon showing tip keys

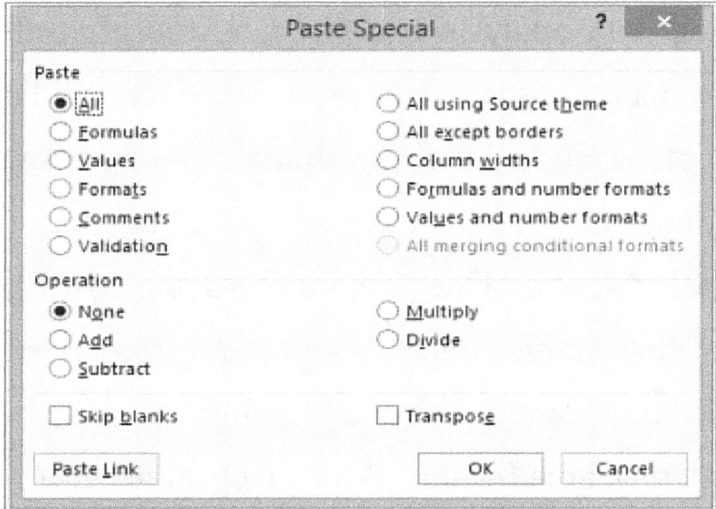

The Paste Special dialog box

Chapter Six

Analysis of Data with Excel

<u>-In Excel, how do you do data analysis?</u>

In Excel, data analysis is a powerful tool that allows users to make sense of large amounts of data and draw meaningful insights from that data. There are several techniques and functions available in Excel that make data analysis easier. One popular method is to use pivot tables. Pivot tables allow users to summarize and analyze large data sets by organizing the data into a more manageable format. With pivot tables, users can easily group, filter, and sort data based on different criteria. This allows them to identify trends, patterns, and outliers in the data set.

Another useful Excel feature for data analysis is the conditional formatting tool. This tool allows users to highlight specific cells or ranges based on certain conditions or rules. For example, users can apply conditional formatting to highlight cells with values above or below a certain threshold. This helps identify outliers or gaps in the data set. Excel also provides various statistical functions such as mean, standard deviation, correlation coefficient, and regression analysis. These functions allow users to perform complex calculations and statistical analyses on their data sets without writing detailed formulas.

Additionally, Excel offers built-in charting tools that allow users to visualize their data through different chart types, such as bar charts, line charts, pie charts, and pie charts. These visual representations help understand the relationships between variables and present results effectively.

Excel offers many features for effective data analysis, including pivot tables to summarize data, conditional formatting to highlight specific cells based on conditions, statistical functions to perform calculations and analysis, and graphical tools for data visualization. By using these tools effectively, users can gain valuable insights from their data sets and make informed decisions based on the results obtained from their analyses.

-How Should the Data Analysis Process Be Conducted?

Data analysis must be done systematically and organised in Excel to ensure accurate results. The first step is to define the goal of the analysis clearly. This involves identifying the problem or question that needs to be answered using available data. Once a goal has been established, collecting and organising relevant data is important. This may involve importing data from external sources or entering data manually into Excel. It is important to ensure the data is complete, accurate, and formatted before performing any analysis.

Different analysis techniques can then be applied to the data depending on the nature of the problem. Excel provides many tools and functions for statistical analysis, such as regression analysis, hypothesis testing, and descriptive statistics. These tools can help discover patterns, relationships, and trends in data. After performing the necessary calculations and analysis, it is essential to interpret and present the results effectively. This may involve creating charts or graphs to visualize trends or summarize results.

It is important to validate and verify the results obtained from Excel by comparing them with other sources or performing sensitivity analysis. This ensures that all conclusions drawn from the analysis are reliable and accurate.

Performing a data analysis process in Excel requires careful planning, organization of data, application of appropriate analysis techniques, interpretation of results, and validation. By diligently following these steps, one can derive meaningful insights from raw data using Excel's powerful analytical capabilities.

-Importance of Data Analysis in Your Business

Data analysis plays a vital role in the success of any business. In today's digital age, businesses generate huge amounts of data daily. This data can provide valuable insights and help make informed decisions to drive growth and profitability.

First, data analytics allows businesses to identify trends and patterns in customer behaviour. By analysing customer data, businesses can better understand their target audience, preferences, and purchasing habits. This information can be used to adjust marketing strategies and product offerings to meet customer needs better, ultimately leading to increased sales and customer satisfaction.

Also, data analytics allows businesses to track key performance indicators (KPIs) and measure the effectiveness of various business processes. By tracking KPIs such as revenue, conversion rates, or customer retention, businesses can identify areas for improvement and make the necessary changes. For example, if data shows sales are down in a particular region or for a particular product line, the company can take corrective action to resolve the problem quickly.

Data analytics helps identify potential risks and growth opportunities. By analyzing market trends and competitor data, businesses can stay ahead of trends and make strategic decisions that give them a competitive advantage. For example, suppose analysis shows that an emerging market segment has high growth potential but low competition. The company can seize this opportunity by developing new products or expanding into that market.

In short, data analytics is essential for any business that wants to thrive in today's competitive landscape. It provides valuable insights into customer behaviour and helps effectively monitor performance metrics while identifying areas for improvement or opportunities for expansion. Therefore, investing in robust data analytics tools and expertise is critical for long-term success.

-The Data Analysis function you should Be Aware of

In today's data-driven world, the ability to analyze and interpret data is becoming increasingly important. Data analysis is an important function that individuals need to know. It includes examining, cleaning, transforming, and modelling data to discover useful insights and make informed decisions. Data analysis is important in various fields, such as business, healthcare, finance, and research. It enables organizations to understand customer behaviour better, identify trends and patterns, detect anomalies or errors, and optimize processes. By analyzing data effectively, businesses can improve decision-making and gain a competitive advantage in the market.

Several methods are used in data analysis, including descriptive statistics, inferential statistics, regression analysis, clustering techniques, and machine learning algorithms. These techniques help summarize large data sets into meaningful information that stakeholders can easily understand.

Additionally, data visualization is integral to data analysis as it helps present complex information visually appealingly. Visualizations like charts, graphs, and dashboards allow users to quickly see patterns and draw conclusions from data.

In short, being aware of the importance of data analytics is essential for those who want to thrive in today's digital age. By understanding this functionality and its various techniques, such as descriptive statistics or machine learning algorithms, along with effective visualization methods, one can harness the power of data to drive informed decision-making across industries.

Chapter Seven

Mistakes' In Microsoft Excel

Microsoft Excel is a powerful tool that allows users to organize and analyze data effectively. However, like any software, it is not immune to errors. Understanding common errors in Excel can help users avoid them and ensure accurate results.

One of the most common errors in Excel is entering a formula or function incorrectly. This can lead to inaccurate calculations and ultimately impact data-driven decision-making. To avoid this, it is important to test formulas thoroughly before applying them.

Another common mistake made in Excel is incorrect formatting. Incorrect cell or column formatting can distort the presentation of data and make it difficult to interpret information accurately. Users should pay attention to cell formats such as dates, currency, and percentages to ensure consistency across spreadsheets.

Ignoring hidden rows or columns can lead to incomplete data analysis. Showing hidden rows or columns is important before calculating or creating a chart.

Finally, neglecting to save your work regularly can lead to significant losses if the program crashes unexpectedly. Saving regularly ensures progress is not lost and avoids unnecessary frustration.

Although Microsoft Excel offers many benefits for effectively organizing and analyzing data, it also has potential errors. Users can minimise these errors by being alert to common errors such as incorrect formulas, incorrect formatting, hidden rows/columns, and infrequent saving habits.

Excel and Daily Life

-Keeping Costs Under Control

In today's rapidly changing business environment, organizations need to control costs. Microsoft Excel is an effective tool that can help achieve this goal. Excel offers many features and functions that allow businesses to track and manage costs effectively. Excel especially helps control costs thanks to its ability to create detailed budgets. By entering different types of expenses and assigning specific amounts, businesses can easily track their expenses against budgeted amounts. This allows any deviations from plans to be identified early, thereby allowing timely corrective actions to be taken.

Excel's built-in formulas and functions make cost-related calculations easier. Whether calculating total costs, average cost per unit, or analyzing cost trends over time, Excel simplifies these tasks by automating the calculations. It not only saves time but also reduces the possibility of human error.

Excel also offers powerful data visualization tools like tables and charts. These visual representations allow businesses to gain insight into their cost models quickly. By visualizing data in an easy-to-understand format, decision-makers can identify areas where costs are increasing rapidly or where there are opportunities for savings.

In short, controlling costs is essential to any organisation's financial health and success. Microsoft Excel provides a comprehensive set of tools that enable businesses to manage costs effectively. Excel allows organisations to control costs in today's competitive business landscape, from creating budgets to performing complex calculations and visualising data.

-Consolidates Data into a Single Place

One of Excel's key features is its ability to consolidate data from multiple sources into one place, giving users a comprehensive view of their information. Excel's Merge feature allows users to consolidate data from different worksheets or workbooks into one central location. This simplifies comparing and analyzing data by eliminating the need to convert between multiple files or worksheets. By unifying data, users can easily identify patterns, trends, and relationships that may not be obvious when working with discrete information.

Consolidating data in one place improves accuracy and reduces errors. Instead of manually copying and pasting data from various sources, Excel's merge feature automates the process, minimizing the risk of human error. This ensures that all relevant information is included while eliminating redundant or duplicate entries. Consolidating data in Excel allows users to perform advanced calculations and easily generate meaningful insights. With all the necessary information collected in one place, users can use Excel's powerful formulas and functions to analyze their data effectively. Whether calculating averages, finding maximum or minimum values, or performing complex statistical analyses, having aggregated data greatly simplifies these tasks.

In summary, consolidating data into one place in Excel brings many benefits to both businesses and individuals. It streamlines the management and analysis process by providing an organized view of information from various sources.

By reducing errors and supporting advanced calculations, this functionality enables users to make informed decisions based on accurate information obtained from unified data sets.

-Access to information Through the Internet

Access to information via the Internet has revolutionized how we collect and analyze data. Microsoft Excel is one of the most powerful tools for organizing and analyzing data. With many diverse functions and features, Excel has become an indispensable tool for professionals in many different fields.

The Internet has made it easier than ever to access information that can be imported into Excel. Thanks to online databases, websites, and search engines, users can find a wealth of data on every topic imaginable. This information can then be easily imported into Excel using built-in import functions. Once the data is in Excel, users have various tools to analyze and manipulate that data. From basic calculations like sums and averages to complex statistical analyses, Excel provides a comprehensive set of functions allowing users to understand their data.

Also, with the advent of cloud computing and online collaboration platforms, multiple users can now view and edit Excel spreadsheets simultaneously. This enables real-time project collaboration, making it easier than ever to collaborate on data analysis and interpretation.

Access to information via the Internet, combined with the power of Microsoft Excel, has changed how we collect, analyze, and interpret data. The ability to import large amounts of data from various sources into Excel provides professionals with a powerful tool to make informed decisions based on accurate analysis. As technology advances, so does our ability to access information over the Internet in programs like Excel.

-It Makes Data Display More Illuminating

Excel is a powerful tool that allows users to organize and analyze data effectively. However, entering data into cells doesn't always produce the brightest display. Excel can use several techniques to make data more attractive and easier to understand. One way to improve data visualization in Excel is to use tables and charts. Users can create visual representations of their data for ease of interpretation by selecting relevant data and choosing the appropriate chart type.

Whether it's a bar chart, pie chart, or line chart, these visual aids can help identify trends and patterns in data. Another technique to consider is conditional formatting. This feature allows users to apply different formatting styles based on specific criteria or conditions. For example, highlighting cells with values above a certain threshold in red or applying a colour scale based on value range can help more easily detect outliers or important information in a large data set.

Using pivot tables can greatly improve the display of complex data sets in Excel. Pivot tables allow users to summarize and analyze large amounts of data by dynamically grouping and classifying information. This lets users quickly generate meaningful information without manually arranging rows and columns.

Making data more visible in Excel involves using various techniques such as tables/charts, conditional formatting, and pivot tables. Using these tools effectively, users can transform raw numbers into visually appealing representations that make the underlying information easier to understand and analyze.

-Security

Excel is a widely used spreadsheet that allows users to store and analyze data. However, with increasing reliance on technology, ensuring the security of sensitive information stored in Excel files is very important. This essay will discuss various security measures that can be implemented to protect data in Excel.

One of the most basic and effective security measures is password protection. By assigning a strong password to an Excel file, unauthorized people cannot access or modify its contents. Combining letters, numbers, and special characters is important for maximum security.

Another way to improve security in Excel is to restrict access to specific cells or ranges in the worksheet. This feature lets users control who can edit or view certain spreadsheet parts while protecting other areas.

Additionally, enabling encryption on Excel files adds an extra layer of security.

Encryption ensures that even if someone gains unauthorized access to the file, they cannot decrypt its contents without the encryption key. Regularly updating and patching Excel software is important in maintaining security. Developers often release updates that patch vulnerabilities and fix bugs, so keeping software current is essential.

Data security in Excel files should be a top priority for anyone using this software.

Implementing password protection, cellular restrictions, encryption, and regular updates can significantly reduce the risk of unauthorized access or data breaches. By taking these precautions seriously, users can ensure that their sensitive information remains secure and confidential in their Excel files.

-Formulate Your Thoughts In Mathematical Terms

Formulating thoughts in mathematical terms in Excel is a powerful tool that allows individuals to organize and analyze data effectively. Excel, a spreadsheet developed by Microsoft, provides a platform for users to enter numeric values and perform various calculations. One of the main benefits of formulating your thoughts in mathematical terms on Excel is the ability to visualize complex data sets. Users can easily identify patterns or trends by entering data into cells and arranging them into rows and columns. It allows them to make informed decisions based on their data analysis. In addition, Excel also provides many mathematical functions that can be applied to data. These functions allow users to perform calculations such as summing values, finding the average, or calculating percentages. By using these functions, individuals can quickly derive meaningful insights from their data without performing each calculation manually.

Excel provides tools for creating tables and charts that visually represent analyzed data. This visual presentation improves understanding and makes it easier to communicate results with others. Overall, formulating thoughts in mathematical terms in Excel allows individuals to analyze and interpret large amounts of data effectively. It promotes logical thinking and problem-solving skills while providing a user-friendly interface for organizing information. Using Excel to form thoughts in mathematical terms proves invaluable in today's data-driven world, whether for personal or professional use.

-Recovering information from spreadsheets and Databases

Microsoft Excel, one of the most widely used spreadsheet programs, offers many features that allow users to store and process large amounts of information effectively. However, problems can still occur despite its user-friendly interface, leading to data loss or corruption. In such cases, knowing how to get information from spreadsheets and databases in Excel is essential.

The first step in recovering lost data is to check your computer's Trash or Trash folder. Frequently deleted files will be temporarily stored here before being permanently deleted. If you find your file in the Trash or Trash folder, simply restore it by right-clicking on it and selecting "Restore" or "Undelete."

If you can't locate your files in the Trash or Trash folder, don't panic! Excel has built-in recovery tools that can help recover lost data. One such tool is the AutoRecover feature, which automatically saves versions of your workbooks periodically. To access this feature, go to the "File" tab and select "Options.

" In the "Save" category, check if AutoRecover is enabled and note the location where recovered files are saved.

Another method for recovering information from Excel spreadsheets and databases is to use backup files. By default, Excel creates a backup of your workbook with the .xlk extension. These backup files are in a designated computer or network drive folder.

If none of these methods successfully recover your lost data, third-party software specializes in recovering damaged or deleted files from Excel spreadsheets and databases. These programs use advanced algorithms to search for recoverable data in damaged files.

To avoid future data loss problems when working with spreadsheets and databases in Excel, it is essential to save your work and create backups regularly.

A cloud storage service or an external hard drive to store important files can provide an extra layer of protection.

Retrieving information from spreadsheets and databases in Excel is an essential skill for anyone who works with data. Users can increase their chances of recovering lost or damaged files by following the above steps. However, prevention is better than cure, so it is essential to adopt good data management practices to minimize the risk of data loss in the first place.

-Make Your Job More Convenient

Excel is a powerful tool that has revolutionized how we handle data and perform calculations in the workplace. With many features and functions, it allows us to streamline our tasks and make our work more convenient. Here are some ways Excel can help improve efficiency and productivity in a workplace.

One of Excel's main advantages is its ability to automate repetitive tasks.

We can perform complex calculations using formulas and functions in just a few clicks. This saves time and reduces the risk of errors when performing manual calculations.

Excel allows us to organize and analyze large amounts of data effectively. With its sorting and filtering capabilities, we can quickly identify patterns or trends in our data sets. This allows us to make informed decisions based on accurate information.

Another feature that makes Excel handy is the ability to create visually appealing charts and graphs. These visual representations help us present our data clearly and concisely, making it easier for others to understand complex concepts or results.

Excel offers different templates that can be customized according to our needs. Whether creating a budget, invoice, or project plan, these templates provide a starting point that saves time and effort.

Excel is a valuable tool that makes our work more practical. Automation capabilities, data organization features, visual presentation options, and customizable templates all help improve efficiency and productivity in the workplace. By effectively harnessing the power of Excel, we can simplify complex tasks and focus on the more important aspects of our work.

-There has been an improvement in time management.

In today's fast-paced world, effective time management is essential for success. With the advent of technology, various tools have been developed to help individuals manage their time effectively. One such tool is Microsoft Excel, a powerful spreadsheet that can be used to improve time management skills. Excel offers many features that can help organize tasks and prioritize activities. By creating a calendar or detailed schedule using Excel, individuals can assign specific periods to each task or activity. It allows for better planning and ensures no tasks are overlooked or forgotten.

Excel allows setting reminders and alerts for important deadlines or appointments. These reminders act as incentives to complete tasks on time, thus preventing procrastination and ensuring productivity.

Another useful feature of Excel is tracking progress and monitoring performance. By entering data related to completed tasks or projects into an Excel spreadsheet, individuals can analyze their performance and identify areas for improvement. This data-driven approach helps identify patterns and trends that can impact productivity positively or negatively.

Excel also allows easy collaboration with colleagues by sharing spreadsheets online. This allows team members to work together simultaneously on a project while keeping track of individual contributions and deadlines.

In summary, using Microsoft Excel as a time management tool offers many benefits, such as improved planning, increased productivity, performance tracking, and effective collaboration. By effectively harnessing the power of this spreadsheet, individuals can improve their overall time management skills and become more successful in their personal and professional endeavours.

-Take a thorough examination of the facts

One of Excel's main strengths is its ability to perform complex calculations and operations. From basic arithmetic to advanced statistical analysis, Excel provides a comprehensive set of formulas and functions that allow users to easily manipulate data. The program offers various data visualization tools, such as tables and charts, that help improve information comprehension.

Another notable feature of Excel is its flexibility in handling large data sets. Users can enter and manage large amounts of data efficiently with a grid structure consisting of rows and columns. In addition, Excel also makes it easy to sort and filter information based on specific criteria.

Excel offers many customization options to meet individual needs. Users can create custom templates or modify existing templates according to their preferences. This flexibility also extends to formatting options; One can choose from various fonts, colours, borders, and designs to enhance the visual appeal of the worksheet. Despite its many advantages, it is important to recognize certain limitations associated with Excel. For example, other specialised software may be more appropriate when dealing with extremely large data sets or complex calculations involving many variables or iterations.

Excel is an essential tool for anyone doing data management or analysis work.

Its various features allow users to organize information efficiently while easily performing complex calculations. However, it is important to recognize the inherent limitations of any software application when considering its use in specific contexts.

-Calculations That Are Bath Quicker and More Accurate

Excel is a powerful tool that has revolutionized calculations in various fields. Its ability to handle complex formulas and large datasets makes it an indispensable tool for professionals across industries.

We will explore how Excel can make calculations faster and more accurate, specifically focusing on its application in the field of baths.

Firstly, Excel provides many built-in functions that simplify complex mathematical calculations. From basic arithmetic operations to advanced statistical analysis, Excel has it all. For example, the SUM function allows for quick addition of multiple cells or ranges, while the AVERAGE function calculates the average value of the selected range. These features eliminate the need for manual calculations, reduce human error, and save valuable time.

Excel's ability to efficiently handle large data sets makes it ideal for bathtub-related calculations. One can easily retrieve specific information from large amounts of data by organizing data in a spreadsheet and using functions like VLOOKUP or INDEX-MATCH. This speeds up the process and ensures accuracy by minimizing human intervention.

Excel's conditional formatting feature allows users to highlight cells based on specific criteria. It is especially useful when analyzing bathtub data, as it allows outliers or trends in the data set to be quickly identified.

Excel offers many benefits when performing tank calculations. Its integrated functions simplify complex calculations, while its ability to process large data sets efficiently ensures accuracy and saves time. By effectively using these features, professionals can improve productivity and make more informed decisions based on reliable bathroom data analysis.

-Improvements in one's ability to analyze information

Excel, the widely used spreadsheet, has revolutionized how we analyze and interpret data. Over the years, several advances have been made to improve the ability to analyze information in Excel. These enhancements simplify complex calculations and provide users with powerful data visualization and manipulation tools.

One of the main improvements is the introduction of advanced formulas and functions. Excel now provides many built-in functions, allowing users to perform complex calculations easily. From basic arithmetic to statistical analysis and financial modelling, these functions save time and effort while ensuring accuracy. In addition, Excel also integrates powerful data analysis tools such as summary tables and charts. Pivot tables allow users to summarize large data sets by creating custom reports and aggregating data based on specific criteria. This feature quickly identifies trends, patterns, and outliers in a data set.

In addition to these analytical features, Excel now supports integration with external databases and online sources. It allows users to import real-time data directly into their spreadsheets for analysis. Connecting to various data sources improves decision-making by providing up-to-date information.

Excel has made significant progress in improving its visibility. Advanced charting options allow users to create visually appealing charts that effectively convey complex information. Adding conditional formatting helps highlight important trends or anomalies in the data set.

In short, improvements in Excel's ability to analyze information have made it an indispensable tool for professionals in every profession. The introduction of advanced formulas, powerful data analysis tools, integration with external sources, and enhanced visualization options have significantly improved its functionality. As technology continues to advance rapidly, we can expect even more exciting developments that will further enhance the ability of individuals to analyze information using Excel effectively.

-Techniques and principles for data visualization

Data visualization is an essential aspect of data analysis because it allows us to present complex information in a visually appealing and easy-to-understand way. Microsoft Excel offers a wide range of tools and techniques that can be used to create effective visualizations. There are some important techniques of data visualization in Excel.

An important principle is simplicity. When creating visualizations, it is essential to keep them simple and uncluttered. Avoid using unnecessary colours, fonts, or elements that distract viewers from the main message. Instead, focus on presenting data clearly and concisely.

Another technique is to choose the appropriate chart type. Excel offers many different chart options, such as bar charts, line charts, pie charts, and scatter charts. Choosing the most appropriate chart type is essential based on the nature of your data and the information you want to convey. Effective labelling plays an important role in data visualization. Labels should be clear, concise, and strategically placed to be easy to read without confusion.

Additionally, proper axis scaling is important for the accurate interpretation of visualizations. Make sure the axis scale matches your data range to make accurate comparisons. Interactivity can improve data visualization in Excel. Use features like filters or slicers to allow users to dynamically explore different aspects of the data.

In summary, one can effectively create Compelling visualisations using Microsoft Excel tools by following these principles and techniques – simplicity, appropriate chart selection, effective labelling, appropriate axis scaling, and interactivity. These visualizations not only make complex information more accessible but also enable better decision-making based on insights gained from analyzing the data presented.

Chapter Eight

Business and Microsoft Excel

Business Analysis

Excel is a powerful tool that has revolutionized the way businesses analyze data. Its wide range of functions and capabilities has become an essential tool for business analysts. This essay will explore how Excel can be used for business analysis.

One of Excel's key features is its ability to process large amounts of data. Business analysts can enter large amounts of data into spreadsheets and use Excel's sort and filter functions to organize and analyze this information. This allows them to identify trends, patterns, and outliers that can provide valuable information for decision-making.

Excel also provides many statistical functions, allowing business analysts to perform complex calculations easily. Excel provides the tools needed for statistical data analysis, from calculating mean and standard deviation to performing regression analysis. Excel's graphical capabilities allow business analysts to present their results visually. They can communicate their analysis clearly and concisely to stakeholders by creating charts and graphs. Excel's pivot tables are another valuable feature for business analysts. Pivot tables allow users to summarize large data sets by grouping and aggregating data based on different criteria. It enables analysts to extract meaningful insights from complex data sets quickly.

Excel is an indispensable tool in business analytics because it processes large amounts of data, performs statistical calculations, creates visual data representations, and uses pivot tables effectively. Its versatility makes it an essential asset for any business analyst seeking accurate information.

People Management

People management is a key aspect of the success of any organization. The popular spreadsheet can be an effective tool for managing people and related tasks. With flexible features and a user-friendly interface,

Excel provides a platform to organize and track various aspects of human resource management.

Excel can make people management easier through employee scheduling. Managers can easily allocate work hours and ensure complete coverage by creating a spreadsheet with columns for dates, shifts, and employee names. It helps avoid conflicts and allows employees to plan their personal lives accordingly.

Excel allows for effective performance tracking. Managers can create spreadsheets with each employee's key performance indicators (KPIs) and update them regularly. This allows managers to track individual progress, identify areas for improvement, and provide constructive feedback during performance reviews.

Excel also facilitates effective communication within the organization. Managers can create forms or surveys that employees can complete electronically using features like data validation or drop-down lists. This streamlines the process of gathering feedback or conducting employee satisfaction surveys.

Excel brings many benefits when managing people in organizations. From planning to performance monitoring and communication support, this software provides a complete solution to manage human resources effectively. Using Excel functions can help improve productivity, better allocate resources, and ultimately contribute to the overall success of an organization's workforce management strategy.

Managing Operations

Excel is a powerful tool that allows individuals to manage operations effectively and efficiently. With many features and functions, it has become a must-have software for businesses, organizations, and individuals. There is some importance in managing activities in Excel and how this importance can benefit users.

One of the main advantages of using Excel for operations management is the ability to manage large amounts of data. With the spreadsheet format, users can enter and organize data in a structured way. This makes it easier to analyze information, identify trends, and make informed decisions.

Excel also provides many different formulas and functions, allowing users to perform complex calculations easily. From basic arithmetic to statistical analysis, Excel offers many tools that simplify data manipulation.

Excel allows for easy collaboration among team members. Multiple users can work on the same spreadsheet simultaneously by saving it to a shared drive or using cloud-based platforms like Microsoft 365 or Google Sheets. This promotes teamwork and improves productivity because everyone can contribute in real-time.

Another advantage of managing operations in Excel is the ability to create reports and visualizations. Users can create tables, charts, pivot tables, and other visual data presentations with just a few clicks. These visuals provide a clear overview of the information and facilitate better understanding for decision-makers.

In short, Excel operations management offers many benefits, such as efficient data management, collaboration capabilities, and visualization tools. It is an essential tool for businesses to streamline their processes and improve productivity. Users can easily manage their operations by leveraging the power of Excel's features and functions.

Reporting

Excel is a powerful tool that allows users to organize and analyze data effectively. One of its key features is the ability to generate comprehensive reports, providing valuable insights into the analyzed data. Creating an Excel report involves many steps, including data collection, analysis, and visualization.

The first step in reporting in Excel is to collect the necessary data. This can be done by importing data from external sources or entering it manually into a spreadsheet. Once data is collected, it must be organized logically for analysis. The collected data can then be analyzed using various functions and formulas available in Excel. These functions allow users to perform calculations, such as adding values or finding the average value.

Additionally, pivot tables can be created to summarize large amounts of data and identify trends or patterns. After analyzing the data, it is important to visualize the results using tables and graphs. Excel provides many charts that can effectively represent different types of information. Users can present their results visually appealing by choosing the appropriate chart styles and formatting options.

Excel reports include collecting and organizing data, analyzing data with functions and formulas, and visualizing results with tables and charts. With flexible features, Excel provides an efficient platform for creating comprehensive reports that provide valuable insights into complex data sets.

Office Administration

Office administration is an essential aspect of any organization, ensuring smooth operations and effective management of resources. In today's digital age, Microsoft Excel has become an indispensable tool for office administrators. With various features and functions, Excel provides a comprehensive platform to streamline administrative tasks.

One of the main areas where Excel excels in office administration is data management. The software allows administrators to organize and manipulate large volumes of data easily. From employee records to financial transactions, Excel allows the creation of structured databases that can be easily sorted, filtered, and analyzed.

Excel provides powerful tools for creating reports and visualizing data. Administrators can create dynamic charts and graphs to present information visually appealingly. This improves understanding of complex data and facilitates the decision-making process.

Another important advantage of using Excel in office administration is the ability to automate repetitive tasks. Administrators can save time by automating calculations, generating invoices or reports, and even sending automated emails using formulas and macros. Excel's collaboration features allow multiple users to work simultaneously on the same spreadsheet. This promotes teamwork among office staff and ensures real-time updates on shared documents.

Microsoft Excel has revolutionized office administration by providing a flexible data management, reporting, automation, and collaboration platform. Its user-friendly interface and powerful features make it an essential tool for modern administrators looking for efficiency and productivity in their daily work.

Strategic Analysis

Excel is a powerful tool that can be used for various purposes, including strategic analysis. The strategic analysis involves evaluating an organization's internal and external environments to identify strengths, weaknesses, opportunities, and threats. Using Excel, analysts can organize and analyze large amounts of data effectively.

One of the main advantages of using Excel for strategic analysis is the ability to handle complex calculations. Analysts can create formulas and functions to calculate profit margin, market share percentage, or ROI. These calculations provide valuable information about an organisation's operational and financial health. Excel allows analysts to create charts and graphs that visually represent data trends. This visual representation allows decision-makers to understand complex information quickly. For example, a line chart can show sales growth over time, or a bar chart can compare market shares between different competitors.

Excel provides tools such as pivot tables that allow analysts to summarize large data sets accurately. Pivot tables allow users to group data by categories and calculate summary statistics such as averages or totals. This feature helps identify patterns or trends that are not obvious when looking at raw data alone.

Excel is an invaluable tool for conducting strategic analysis because of its ability to handle complex calculations, create visual representations of data trends, and summarize large data sets effectively. By effectively using these features, organizations can make informed decisions based on accurate and comprehensive analysis.

Project Management

Project management is important to any organization, ensuring tasks are completed efficiently and on time. Although many project management tools are available, Excel remains popular due to its flexibility and user-friendly interface. With powerful features and customizable options, Excel provides an effective platform for project management.

One of the main benefits of using Excel for project management is the ability to create Gantt charts. These charts visually represent project timelines, allowing managers to track progress and identify potential bottlenecks. Excel automatically creates a Gantt chart outlining the project timeline by entering deadlines and task dependencies.

Additionally, Excel's spreadsheet format allows for easy data entry and manipulation. Project managers can create comprehensive task lists, assign responsibilities, set deadlines, and track progress in one place. This centralized approach helps streamline communication between team members and ensures everyone is on the same page.

Excel also provides a variety of formulas and functions that enhance project management. For example, managers can use conditional formatting to mark overdue or important tasks. Additionally, they can use formulas like SUMIF or COUNTIF to calculate resource allocation or monitor budget usage.

Although specialized project management software exists today, Excel remains a reliable tool for effective project management. The ability to create Gantt charts, facilitate data entry and manipulation, and leverage powerful formulas makes it an invaluable asset to any organization looking to solve problems.

Managing Programs

Excel is a powerful tool that can be used to manage programs effectively. With many features and functionalities, it provides a comprehensive platform to organize and track various aspects of the program. Whether it's budgeting, planning, or resource allocation, Excel can handle it all.

One of the main benefits of using Excel for program management is the ability to create custom spreadsheets. This allows program managers to design templates that suit their needs and requirements. They can include tasks, deadlines, responsible parties, and progress updates columns. By entering relevant data into these spreadsheets, managers can easily track the status of each task and identify bottlenecks or issues that need attention.

Excel's built-in formulas and functions enable automated calculations and analysis. For example, a manager can use a formula to calculate the total budget allocated to a program or determine the completion percentage for each task. These calculations provide valuable information about the program's progress and help make informed decisions. In addition to managing tasks and budgets, Excel facilitates effective communication between team members.

By sharing spreadsheets via cloud-based platforms or email attachments, everyone involved in the program can access real-time information about project updates or changes. This ensures transparency and collaboration within the team.

Excel program management offers many benefits, including customization options, automatic calculations, and advanced communication capabilities. It streamlines program management processes by providing an organized platform for tracking tasks, budgets, deadlines, and progress updates. Therefore, using Excel as a program management tool is highly recommended for effective program planning and implementation.

Contract Administration

Contract management is an essential aspect of project management, ensuring that all parties involved comply with the terms and conditions outlined in the contract.

Excel, a widely used spreadsheet, offers many benefits for effective contract management. This essay explores the benefits of using Excel for contract management.

First, Excel provides a structured and organized platform for storing and managing contract data. It allows users to create customizable templates with predefined fields like project details, deliverables, milestones, payment schedules, etc. This standardized format ensures consistency and easy access to essential information.

Second, Excel's calculation functions enable accurate financial tracking throughout the contract lifecycle. Users can generate real-time reports on budget usage or outstanding payments by entering relevant data, such as expenses incurred or payments received. These calculations allow you to identify potential gaps or problems quickly.

Excel's sorting and filtering capabilities allow users to track deadlines and track progress effectively. Features like conditional formatting and colour-coding options make seeing upcoming tasks or overdue activities easier.

Excel facilitates collaboration among team members by allowing multiple users to access and update the same document simultaneously. This feature streamlines communication between stakeholders involved in contract management.

Using Excel for contract management offers several benefits, including structured data storage, accurate financial tracking, effective deadline-tracking tools, and collaboration. By effectively leveraging these benefits through appropriate training and the use of advanced Excel spreadsheet features, we can significantly improve the efficiency of the contract management process.

Chapter Nine

Practical

Let's start by entering some data. Click into cell A1 and type in a header sales. To move over to the next cell, click on it with the mouse, or you could also press the tab or the right arrow key on your keyboard, and that'll move over to the next cell, and we will type in a date as the second header. To move down, press the down arrow key or press enter.

For example, assuming we work for a cookie company and want to track cookie sales starting in January 2023. We type in January 2023 and then hit enter. That's the first month, and it will track through November 2023.

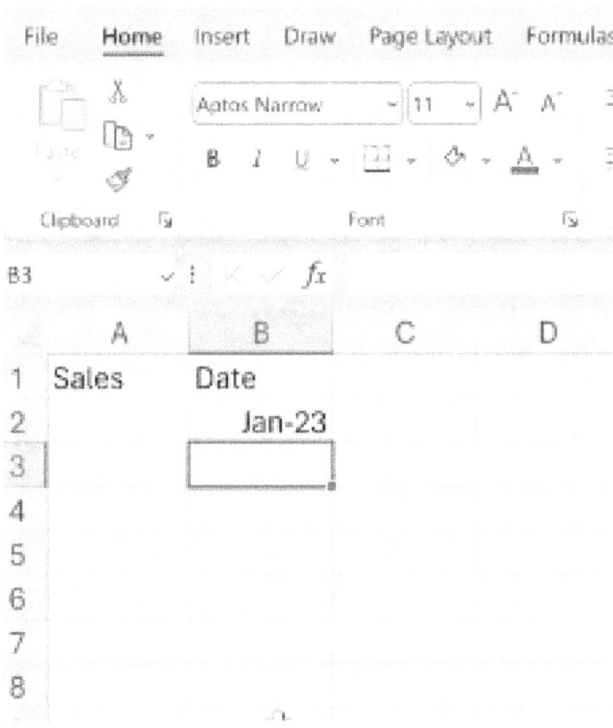

You could type in every month, but Excel is smart and detects a pattern. When you click into cell B2, notice a rectangle in the bottom right-hand corner; the cursor changes when you hover over it. Press and hold on to that and drag it down to fill in all the different months.

This method works with dates and numbers as long as Excel can detect a pattern.

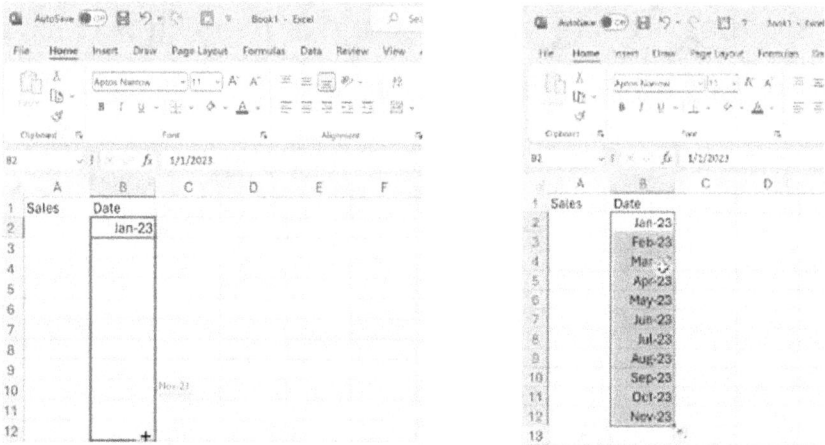

Next, enter data on how many cookies are sold. January is by far the worst month for the cookie business. Go through and fill in the numbers for the rest of the months. When done filling in the numbers, It's a little difficult to parse them at a glance.

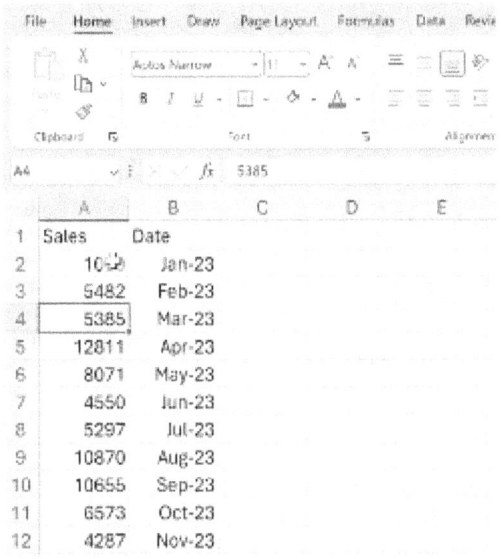

Highlight all the cells, and up on the home tab within the home ribbon in the centre, click the comma-style icon to add a thousand separators. That makes it much easier to tell which numbers are larger or smaller.

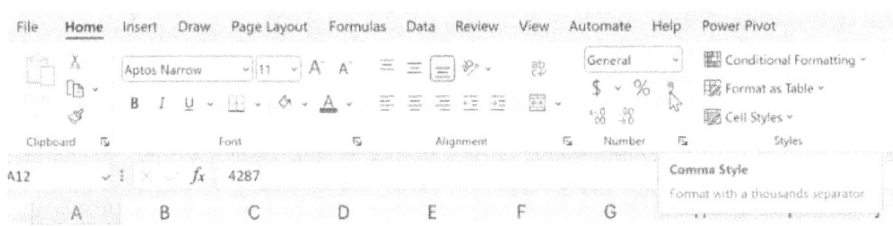

If you don't need decimal places in your numbers, go to the top, click on numbers, and you can remove the decimal places.

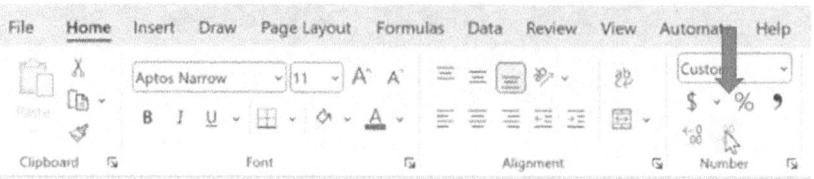

Now, as a neat little pro tip, press Control + 1 on your keyboard, opening up the format cells dialogue. There, you have full control over what the format of the cell is. At the table, you can provide some context for why January was such a low sales month. Click into cell C1 and add another header titled Notes. In C2, provide an explanation like New Year's resolution depresses sales.

	A	B	C	D	E	F
1	Sales	Date	Notes			
2	1,000	Jan-23	New Year's resolution depresses sales			
3	5,482	Feb-23				
4	5,385	Mar-23				
5	12,811	Apr-23				
6	8,071	May-23				
7	4,550	Jun-23				
8	5,297	Jul-23				
9	10,870	Aug-23				
10	10,655	Sep-23				
11	6,573	Oct-23				
12	4,287	Nov-23				
13						
14						

The explanation bleeds over into the adjacent columns, and ideally, it should fit within column C. Click on the line between C and D and double click, and that'll auto-fit the contents to expand C. If you have many different columns or rows that you would like to fit into the content, click on the page number icon and click on any line between the two columns to auto-fit. It's a handy little trick.

	A	B	C
C4			f_x
1	Sales	Date	Notes
2	1,000	Jan-23	New Year's resolution depresses sales
3	5,482	Feb-23	
4	5,385	Mar-23	
5	12,811	Apr-23	
6	8,071	May-23	
7	4,550	Jun-23	
8	5,297	Jul-23	
9	10,870	Aug-23	
10	10,655	Sep-23	
11	6,573	Oct-23	
12	4,287	Nov-23	
13			

On column C, right-click, which shows you a context menu with different actions you can take. You can delete or hide a column, but it doesn't remove the data. It's just hidden on the sheet. To show the hidden column again, highlight the two columns, right-click, and unhide. You can also do that with rows as well.

From our data, we can show the date first, followed by the sales. The good news is that it's very easy to move columns in Excel. Highlight all the data, press the shift key on the keyboard, hover over the edge, and the cursor changes. Press the left mouse button and move the column to a new position. You can place it to the left of sales to place the date first.

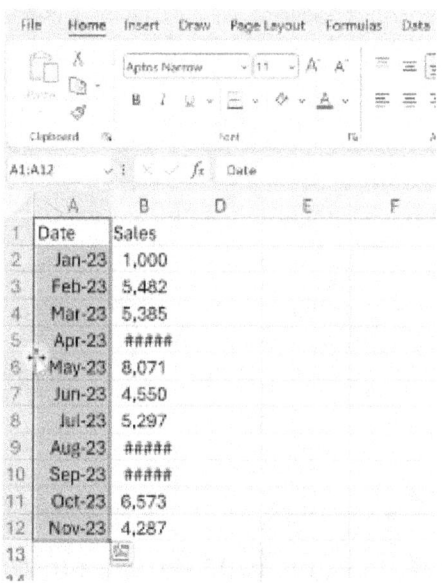

You can format the table to look better. Go to the top tabs and click Insert to insert a table. It automatically identifies all the data and then click OK. Now, you will have banded rows, and reading the table is much easier.

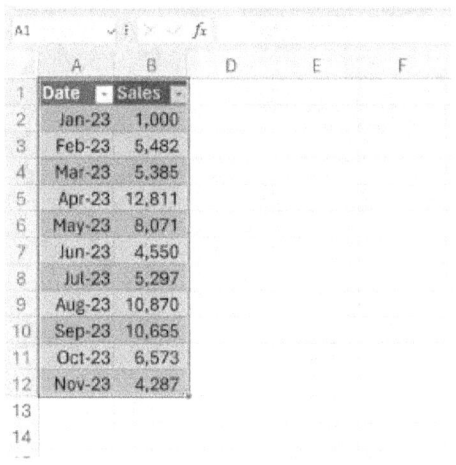

You have different styles under the table design on the right-hand side or stick with the default. The benefits of tables go beyond just the look and feel. You could also add a total row to see the total down at the bottom. Click on the little dropdown arrow beside the total cell. Choose what you want to total up. For example, sum up all the sales in this case.

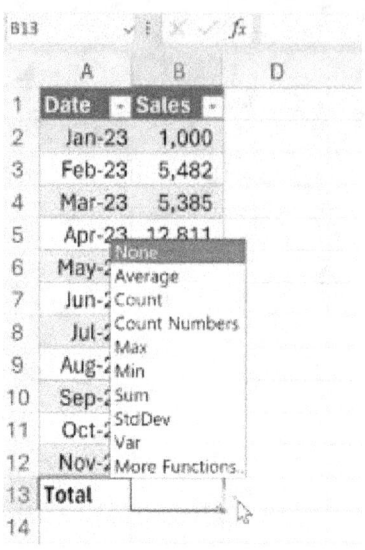

Highlight all the cells, and there's conditional formatting on the home tab in the centre, which allows you to format the cells based on a condition or the underlying data and have different options. You could choose data bars and colour scales and define your rules.

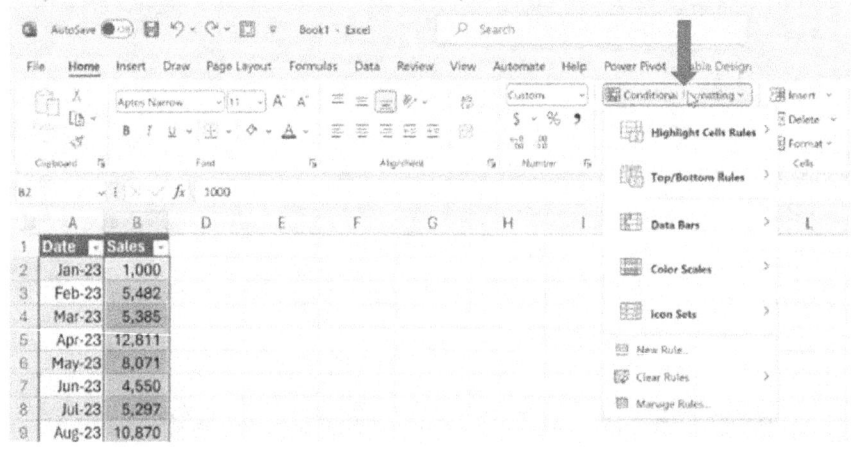

Click on colour scales and apply red for lower and green for higher numbers. When you look at the data, you can quickly tell that December was by far the best month of the year.

	A	B	D
	Date	Sales	
1	Date	Sales	
2	Jan-23	1,000	
3	Feb-23	5,482	
4	Mar-23	5,385	
5	Apr-23	12,811	
6	May-23	8,071	
7	Jun-23	4,550	
8	Jul-23	5,297	
9	Aug-23	10,870	
10	Sep-23	10,655	
11	Oct-23	6,573	
12	Nov-23	4,287	
13	Dec-23	23,52	
14	Total	98,505	
15			

B13 fx 23524

Data Analysis

Let's start analyzing the data; luckily, Excel makes that easy. First, know the total sales in Q1. So, from January through March, you can simply highlight the three cells, and at the right side bottom of your table, you have the status bar. There, you can see the total sales of the Q1.

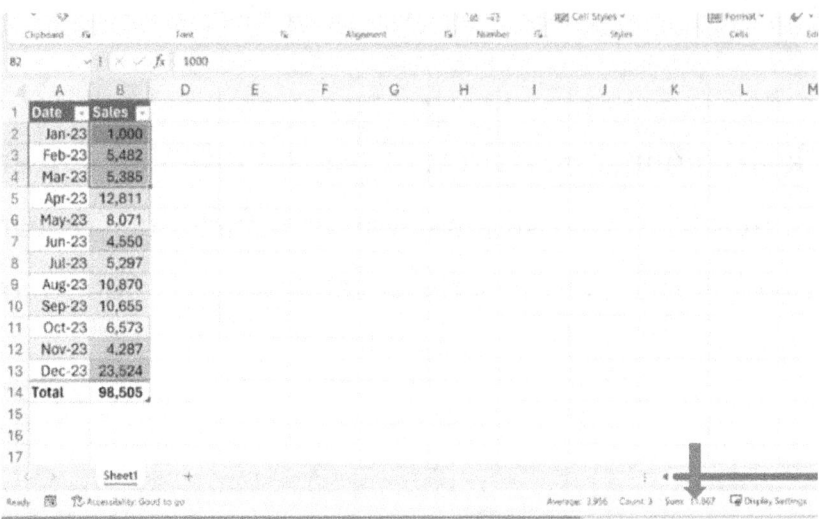

Go to the home tab and click analyze data on the right-hand side. That opens up the analyze data panel, and the really neat thing is that you can simply ask questions about your data, and Excel will provide insights. If you ask what is the total sales in Q1 and request to see that as a table, Excel will provide you with that. That makes analysis easy; you don't have to enter a function or formula.

You can also calculate that on your own. Click down into the cell and add up Q1. Enter the equal sign, letting Excel know you're about to enter a formula. Next, click on cell B2; you will see it in the formula. Enter the plus sign to cell B3 and add that to cell B4. Press enter, and you also see that the total was 12,000. Along with addition, you could also do subtraction, multiplication, and division.

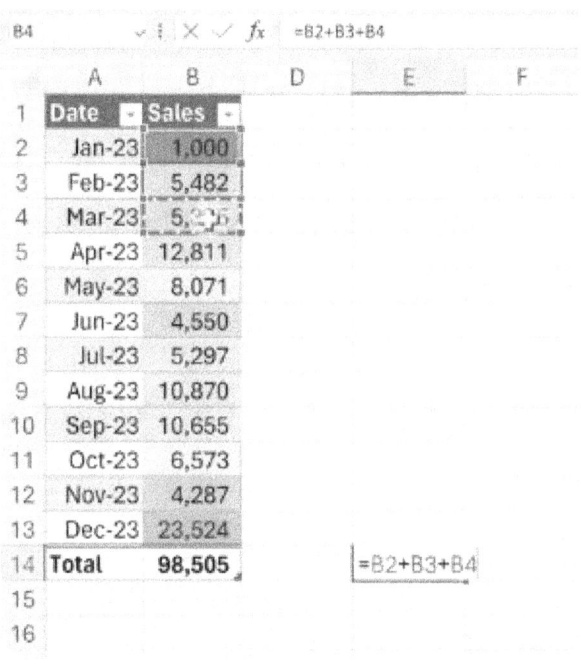

Alternatively, you can use a function. One of the most popular functions is "SUM." Again, enter the equal sign and type in the function name, "SUM." Then, open the parenthesis and pass in an argument or all the numbers you want to summarize by highlighting the cells, closing the parenthesis, and hitting enter.

Excel has many functions available. At the very top, click on the Formulas tab, and under AutoSum, you have some of the most popular functions you might want to use.

We've just been working with all the data in a tabular format, but sometimes, a picture or a chart is worth a thousand words. Go to the Insert tab on top; in the center, you can choose Charts. You could insert a recommended chart or choose one of the many different options. Click on Recommended Charts, and it recommends a line chart that works well with your data type. Click OK, and that inserts a chart.

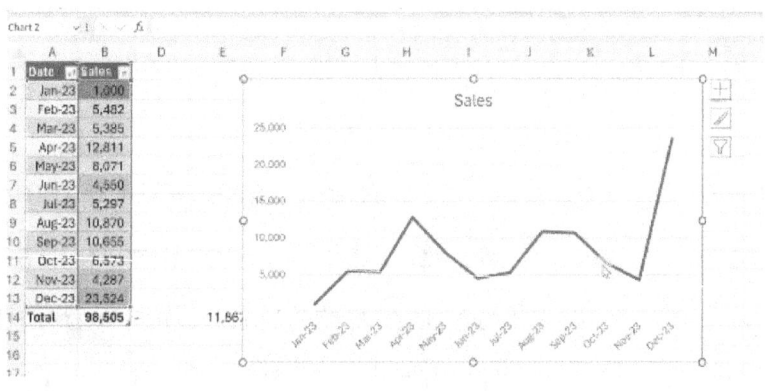

Now, you can visually see what sales were like throughout the year. That's a lot easier to parse the data. On the top, you have all sorts of tools that can customize how the chart looks.

Chapter Ten

Python in Excel

This section will explain how to use Python directly within Microsoft Excel. If you've never heard of Python, it's a powerful and popular programming language that supports data manipulation and visualization, statistical modelling, machine learning, etc.

You can take advantage of these different capabilities by bringing Python into Excel. It turbocharges Excel. We will start with the basics of using Python in Excel and then look at more advanced scenarios.

In Microsoft Excel, there are a few different ways to access Python. First, go to the top tabs and click on formulas.

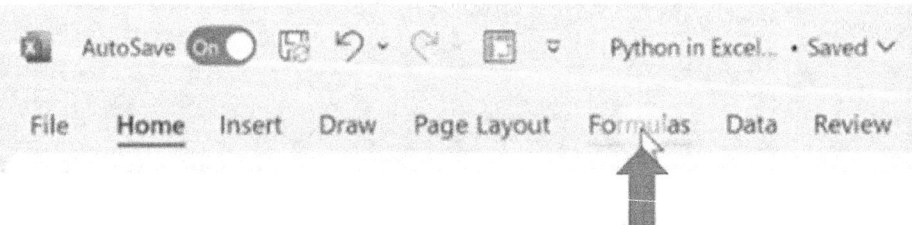

In the center of the ribbon, there's now a new category titled Python, and you can insert Python code there. Click on the icon and notice that a few things have changed on the screen.

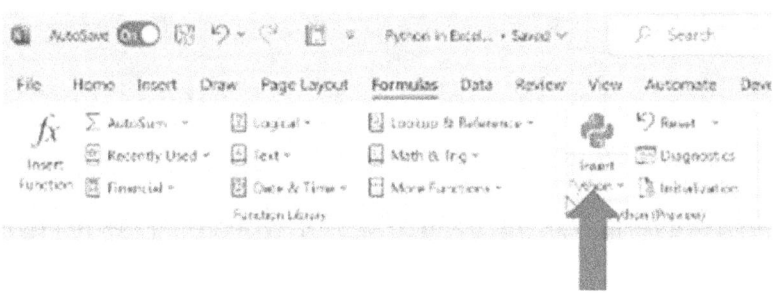

Within the formula bar, you now have the PY icon. That indicates that you can enter Python code. Also, at cell A1, you'll see the PY. Enter the code directly into cell A1. With Excel, there are many different ways to insert Python code.

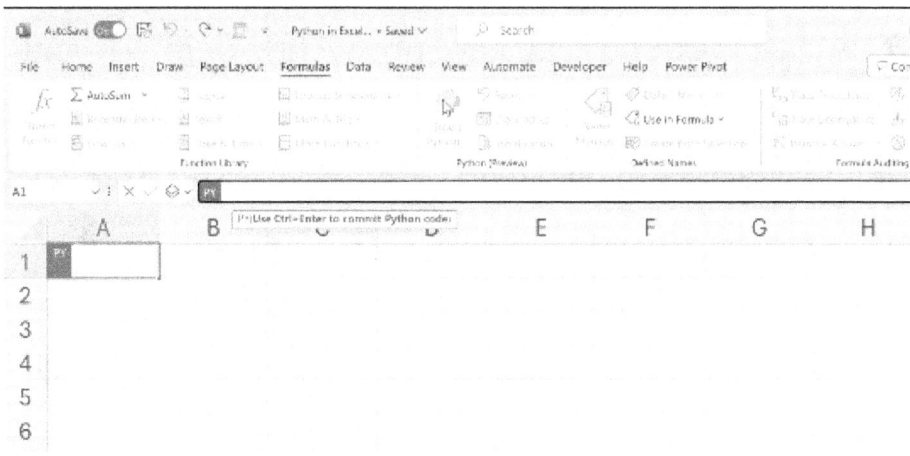

You can also simply enter a function. Type in "=PY,"
then open parenthesis, which activates Python mode.
You will see the icon again in the formula bar and the
cell. You can also use a shortcut key: press Ctrl, Alt,
Shift, and P, which activates Python mode.

If you have Python enabled, start entering some code.
You can enter Python code directly into the cell or enter
code directly into the formula bar above. The formula
bar is a multi-line editor, but you can only see one line.

To give more space on the formula bar, click the
dropdown arrow on the right-hand side, which exposes
a few more lines. You can collapse it in the dropdown
or click on the dividing line to expand or collapse it.
Now, a quick shortcut key: press Ctrl, Shift, U, and
that'll expose more lines, and when you press it again,
it'll toggle back to one line.

Now start entering some code. For example, let's say
"Hello World" in Python. Insert a quote, type in "Hello
World," close out the quotes, and press Enter. When

you press Enter, it doesn't do anything; it just inserts a new line within the multi-line editor.

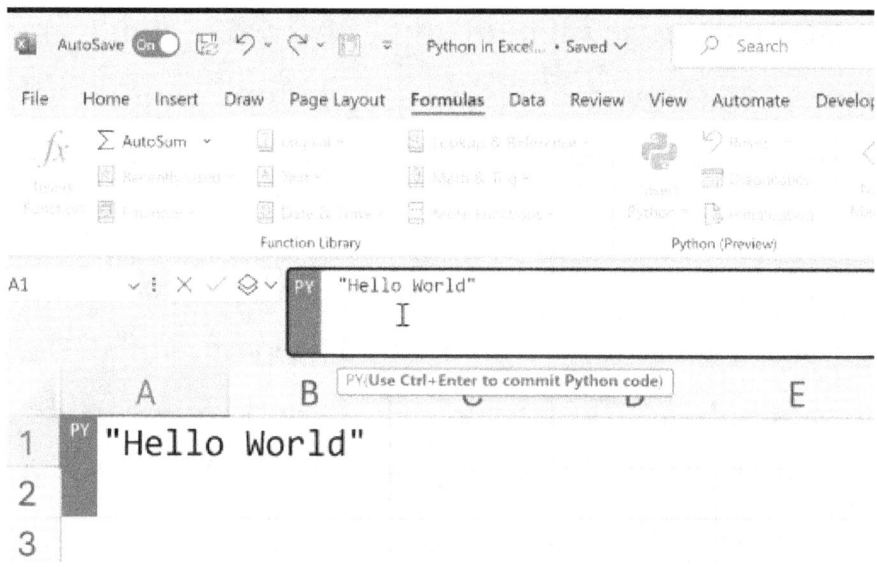

To commit the Python code, notice the tooltip that says press Control and Enter. So, press control, enter, and it says Hello World in the cell to write your first Python code in Excel.

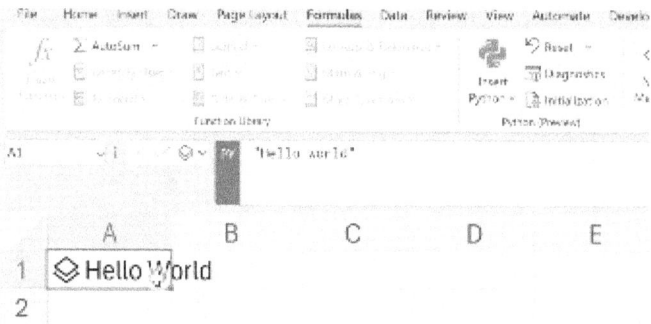

You will notice that when you press control and enter, cell A1 briefly says busy before showing the result Hello World, and you might wonder why. The reason is that the Python code runs in the Microsoft cloud on Microsoft servers. It doesn't run on your local computer. So, it causes a slight delay. You might think that's a disadvantage, but having Python run on Microsoft servers means you don't have to install Python on your local computer and keep track of all the different Python versions. So, it works out to be somewhat of an advantage. Click into another cell, cell C4, and enter more Python code.

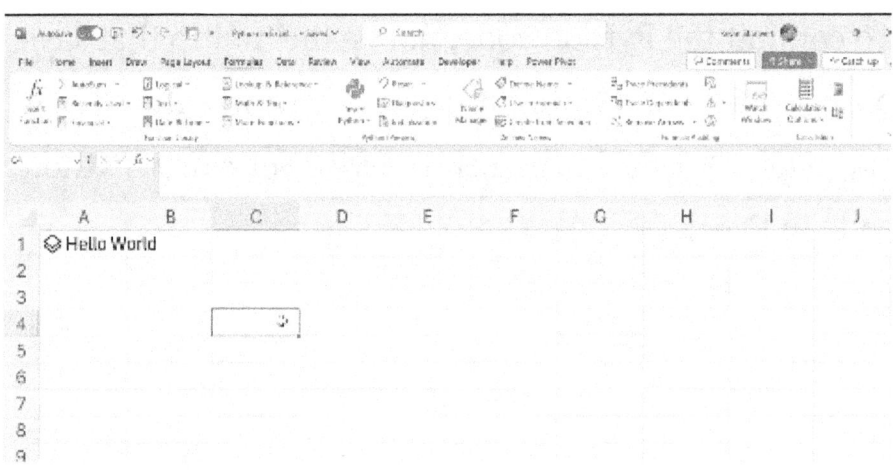

Again, go up to formulas and then click on Insert Python. Enter a variable name, and let's call it chocolate chip. A variable is a container, and you can assign a value to that container. So, let's set chocolate chip = 3.

Then, to commit that, press control, enter, and you have 3.

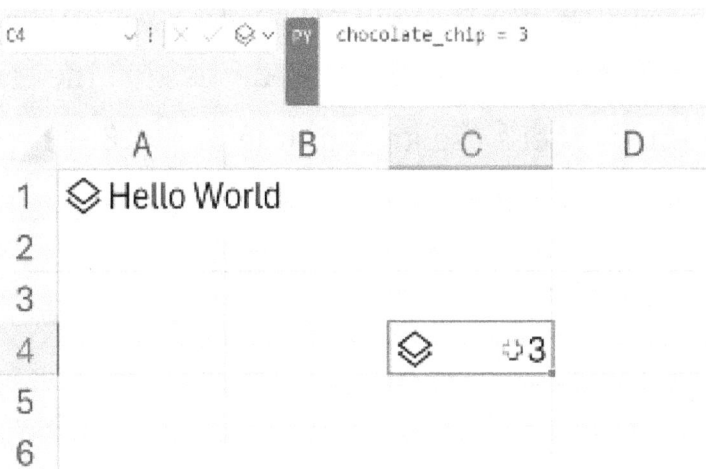

With Python, you always get the last result back in the cell. Assuming you add one more variable. let's type in oatmeal raisin = 2. press control, enter and in cell C4, you see 2.

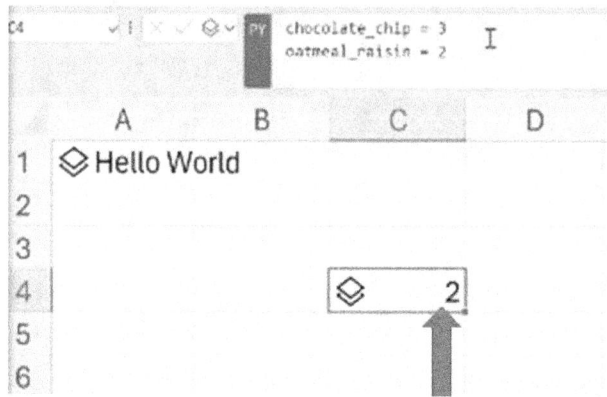

So, what happened to the chocolate chip cookie? Again, Excel will only show the last result from Python. In this case, it happens to be oatmeal raisin, and you have 2. You can now reference the variables throughout your workbook; the Python code is in the same environment. Let's use an example in cell B6: Type in total cookies to make that real.

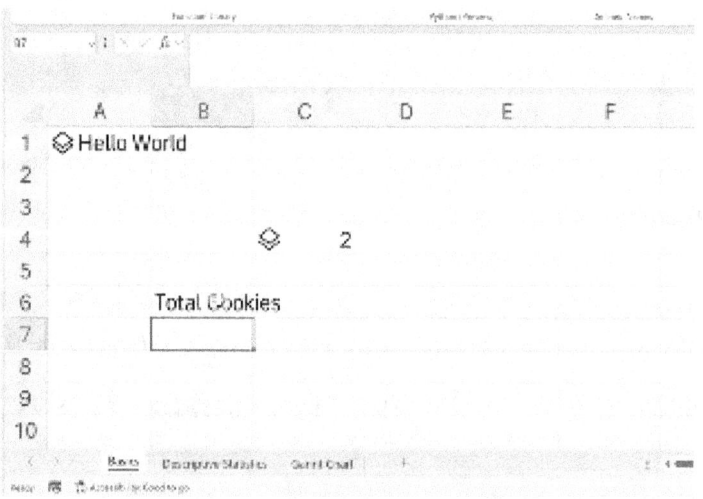

Adjust the column width and click into cell C6. Again, insert some more Python code. You can create a new variable called total cookies and set it equal to chocolate chip plus oat. Then press control, enter, and that commits the code. That takes the value of chocolate chip and oatmeal raisin from the Python code in a different cell. That's pretty powerful.

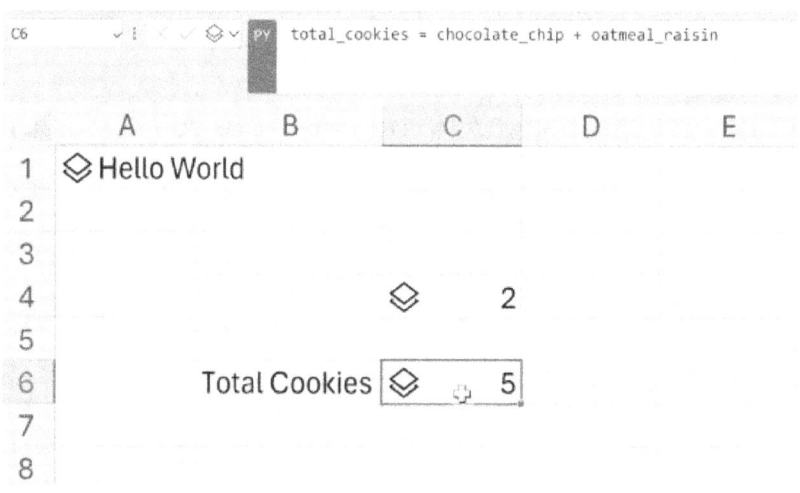

You need to be aware that the position of your Python code makes a difference. Click into cell C6, press control X to cut that, move it up to cell C3, and paste. When you move from cell c6 to c3, the pane opens up on the right-hand side with an error message. The pane on the right-hand side is similar to a console in an IDE.

Another way to get to the pane. Go to formulas, click on diagnostics, and there again, you will see the error message.

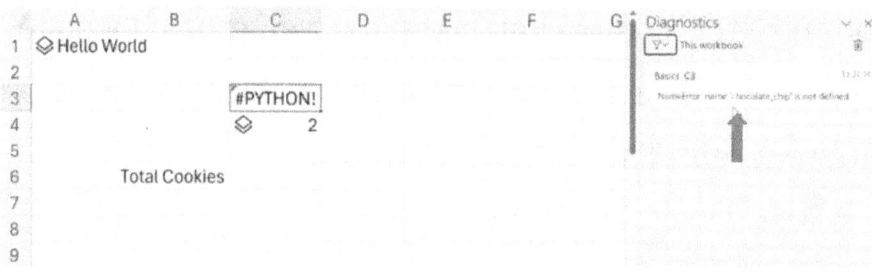

Why the error message? If you click into cell C4, define "chocolate chip." Excel first runs the Python code before you define any of the values, so there is an error message back. Excel runs Python code as follows: it first evaluates the code from the leftmost position to the rightmost position. Then, it works its way down the sheet and progresses from the leftmost worksheet to the rightmost worksheet.

One thing to keep in mind is, let's say that you're importing data or you're defining values. It makes sense to do that in the leftmost, topmost position on your leftmost worksheet, and then you can use that throughout all your other worksheets within the workbook. So far, you have been assigning all the variables directly in the Python code, but you can also use values directly from your Excel sheet.

In cell B5, let's type in "sugar cookies" and say we just have one of them. The total Cookies only show "chocolate chip" + "oatmeal raisin," so we need to add "sugar." When you click on cell C5 for "sugar," you'll notice that it added an "XL," then it has cell C5. It takes in data directly from the Excel sheet using the function. Press Ctrl + Enter to get the total result of the cookies, which is 6.

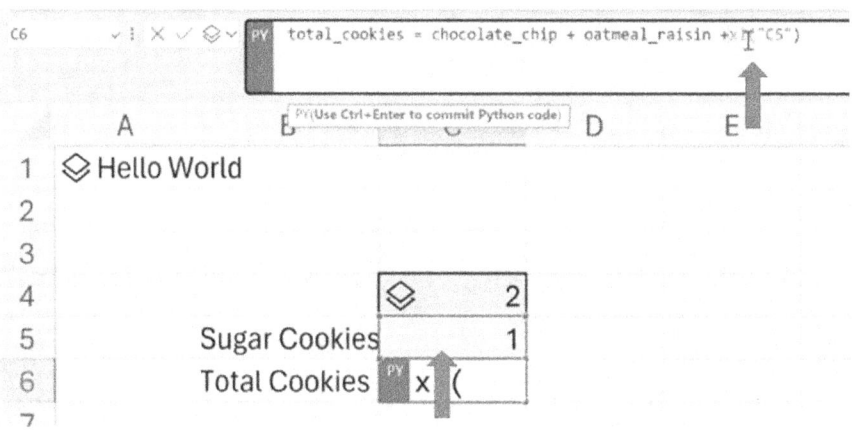

You can work with the results of the Python code anywhere in your Excel workbook. It recalculates all the different Python code on the sheet, especially if you have much code that could slow things down.

You have calculation options on the top tabs under formulas on the right-hand side. Click on that, and if it is set to automatic, it means that whenever you hit enter or control enter, it'll go through and run all the different calculations. You can also set it to partial, where it'll continue to evaluate all your different Excel formulas but not your Python code, or you could set it to manual, where you have to go through and calculate.

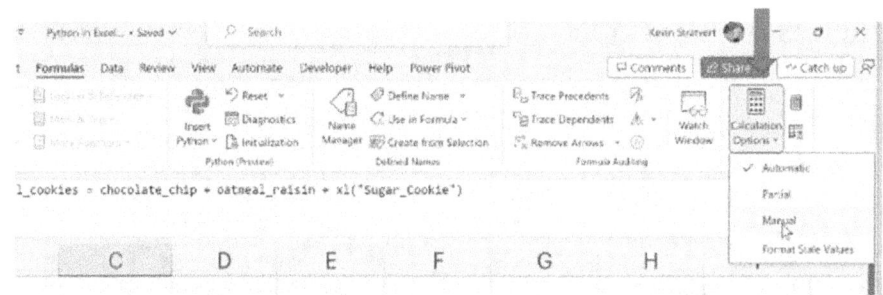

As we've been walking through these different examples, one thing that might have stood out is an icon next to the Python code result. If you click on the icon, that shows more information about the result. That is referred to as a Python object.

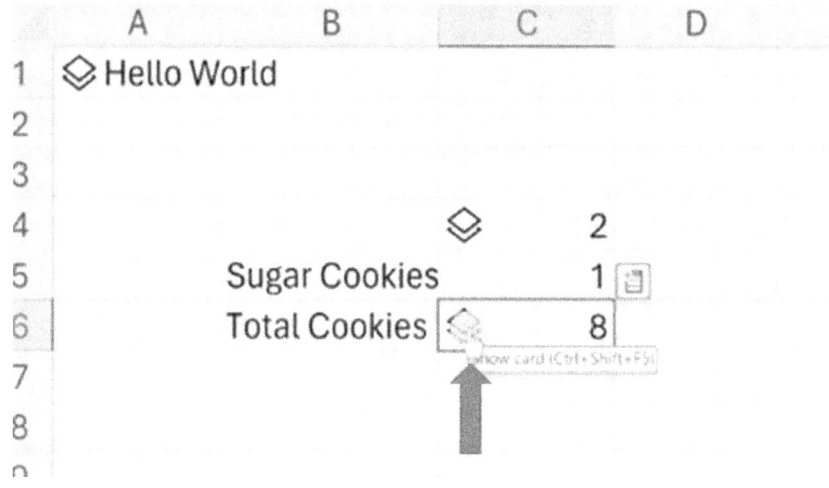

You can have an output as a standard Excel value and toggle between those types with a keyboard shortcut. Press control, alt, shift, and M, and that'll shift back to a Python object, and when you press control, alt, shift, and M, that shifts it back to an Excel result.

Let's go to the next descriptive statistics worksheet to see how it can make a difference. You have a table with some cookies and the associated quantity on the descriptive statistics worksheet.

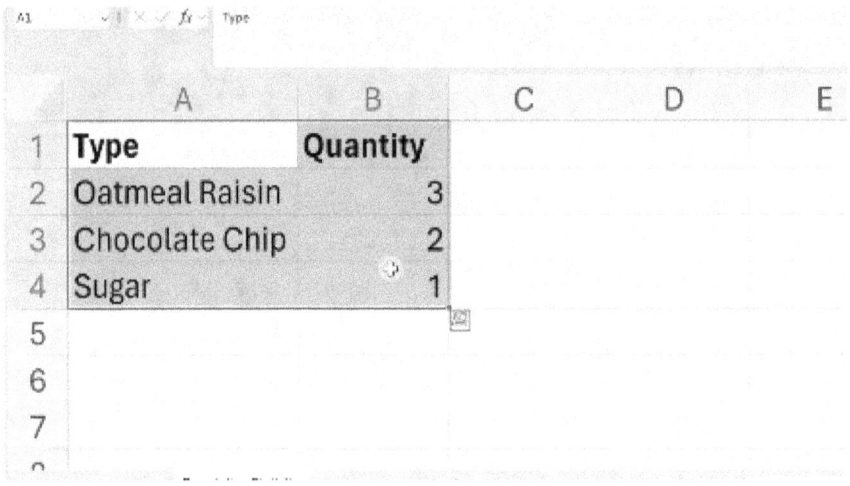

	A	B	C	D	E
1	Type	Quantity			
2	Oatmeal Raisin	3			
3	Chocolate Chip	2			
4	Sugar	1			
5					
6					
7					

Click into cell A6 and insert some Python code. Click on the Python icon and enter the variable cookie table. Set it equal to the previous table. Again, you have the function XL, which takes the range and automatically identifies that you have headers.

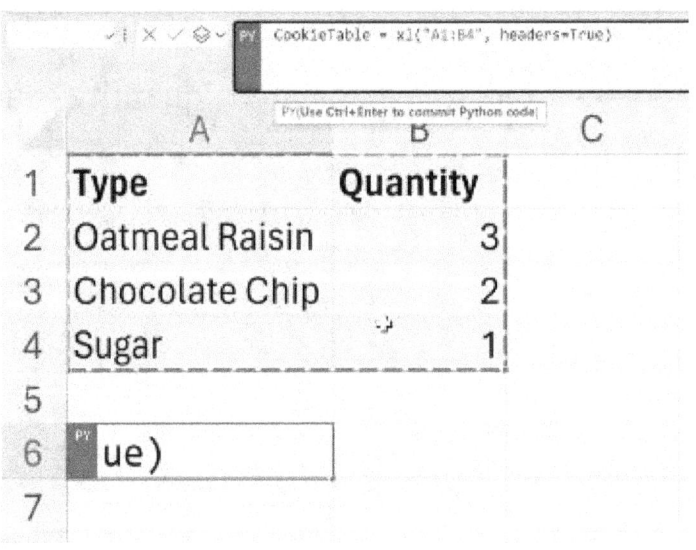

Press control and enter to bring up the data frame, a Python object.

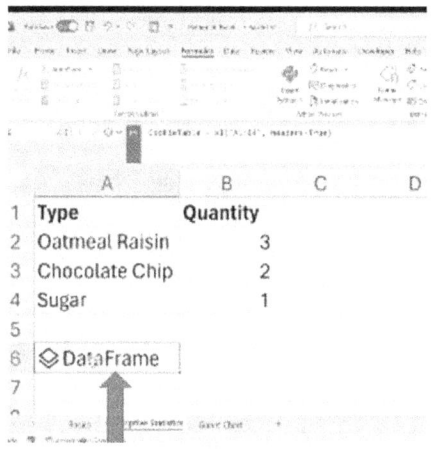

Right-click on the object, and there's the option to show the data type card. When you click on that, you have all the different contents. Now, you might be wondering what is a data frame. It's very similar to a table that contains data. If you want to expand it just like a standard Excel table, go up, click on the dropdown, and instead of outputting it as a Python object, you can output it as an Excel value. You have your table and all the data when you click on Excel value. It takes up a little bit more space.

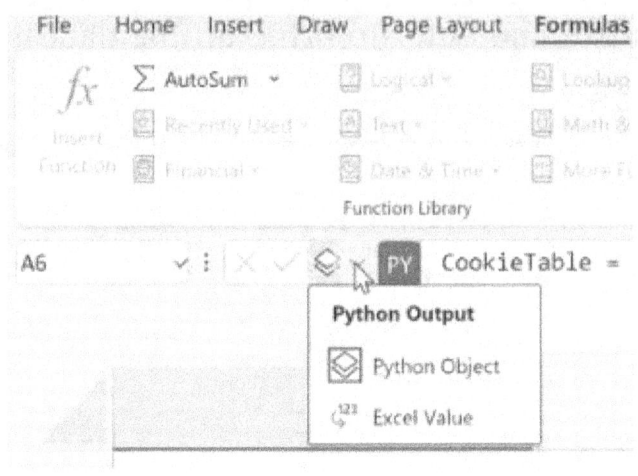

If you don't want to see all the data and want to store it in the data frame, click on the dropdown on the top and select the Python object. The data will be all contained within one individual cell.

In this example, we built a data frame using a very simple data table directly on the worksheet, but you can pull in data from just about anywhere. It could be SQL Server, from Azure, from a CSV file.

On the top, Click on the data tab, and over on the left-hand side, click on Get data from just about anywhere using Power Query. Once you import the data, you can assign it to a data frame and use it with Python.

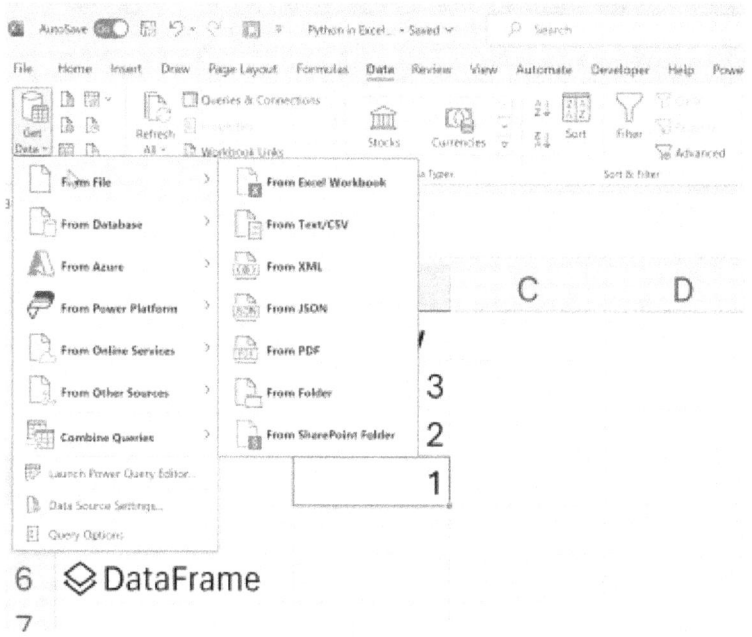

So far, we've been looking at some basic uses of Python, but many of Python's powers come from using different Python libraries. On the top tabs, click on formulas. In the centre, you have the Python group. Click on the option that says initialization. That opens up a pane on the right-hand side, and as part of Python, you get all the different libraries. You can import NumPy, Pandas, Matplot, Statmodels, and Seaborn. Some of these help you with analysis and visualization.

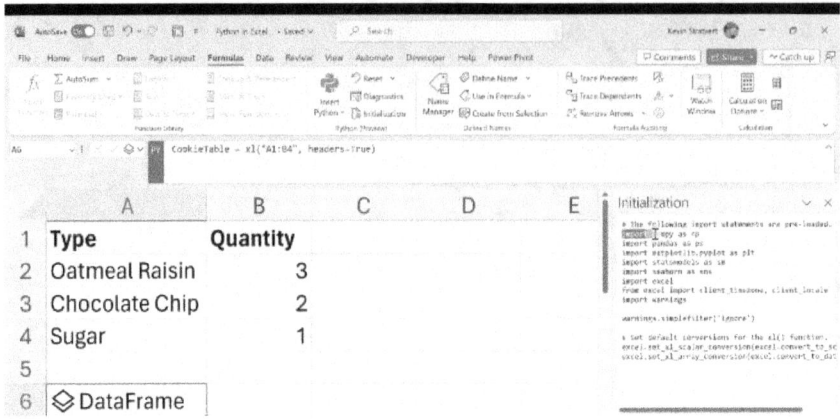

Let's say you want to work with PyTorch JSON, LTK, or regex, and you can also import them. Within your Python code, simply type in the import, and then you can type in PyTorch, which will load the library, and you can now use that as part of your analysis and visualization.

Chapter Eleven

Gantt chart

This section will explain how to create a super simple Gantt chart in Excel. A Gantt chart is frequently used in project management to track the progress of a project.

In Excel, let's assume you are working with a Cookie Company and want to bake chocolate chip cookies, which involves several steps and tasks.

Using the image below as an example, column A lists all the tasks required to make that happen. Column B lists the dates to kick off all the different tasks. Column C provides an estimate of how many days each task will take. We have the completion date in column D, but you'll notice it's not simply taking the start date and adding the days needed. It's a little farther out because we assume work is not done during weekends.

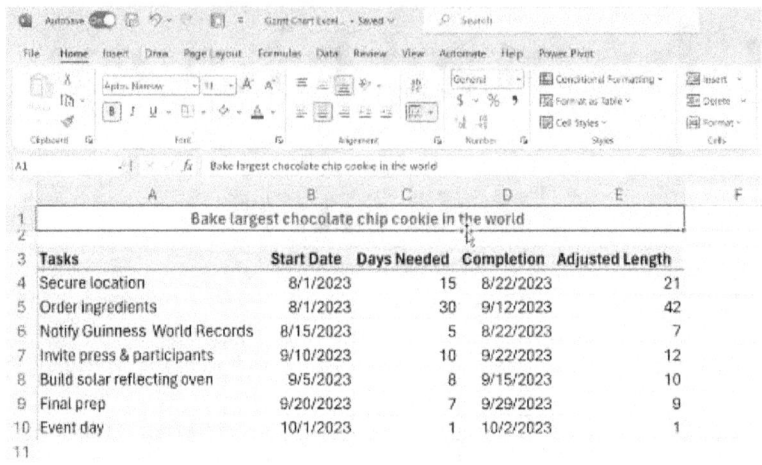

To calculate the completion date, use a function called workday, and you can see that at the top. Click on the function helper to open up the function arguments with two required arguments. The two arguments are in bold.

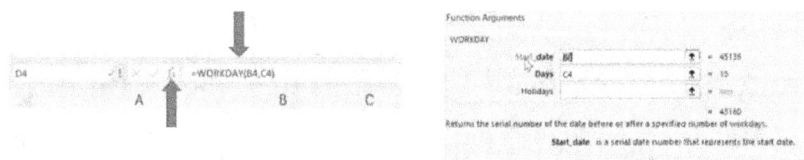

Enter the start date for the first task as B4. Next, indicate how many days the task will take as cell C4, which is 15 days. Next is an optional argument. You can indicate if there are any holidays, but if not, you can leave them blank and then click OK.

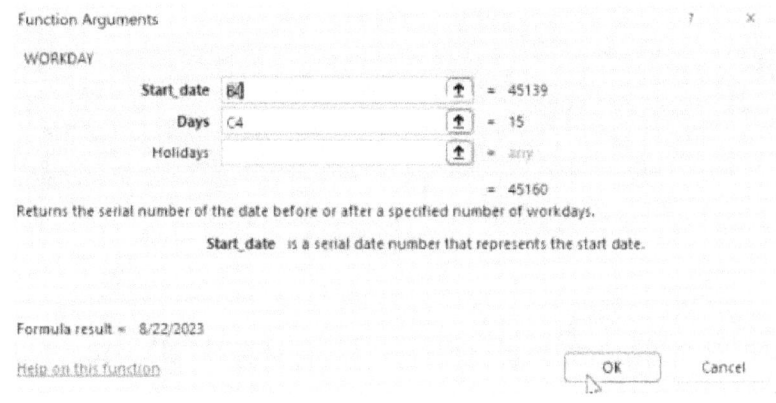

That shows the completion date, which determines how many days it'll take and includes all weekends. Now that you have the completion date, you need to calculate the adjusted length that factors in weekends, which is simple. Take the completion date as cell D4 and subtract cell B4 or the start date, which tells you the adjusted length.

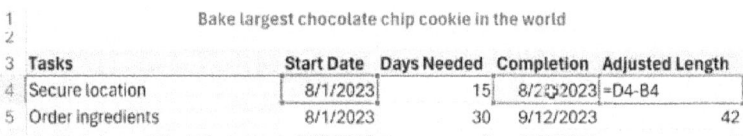

1		Bake largest chocolate chip cookie in the world		
2				
3	Tasks	Start Date	Days Needed	Completion	Adjusted Length
4	Secure location	8/1/2023	15	8/22/2023	=D4-B4
5	Order ingredients	8/1/2023	30	9/12/2023	42

Applied the same formula to all the different cells, and your data table is all set. You need to make one modification to get a stacked bar chart.

Tasks	Start Date	Days Needed	Completion	Adjusted Length
Secure location	8/1/2023	15	8/22/2023	21
Order ingredients	8/1/2023	30	9/12/2023	42
Notify Guinness World Records	8/15/2023	5	8/22/2023	7
Invite press & participants	9/10/2023	10	9/22/2023	12
Build solar reflecting oven	9/5/2023	8	9/15/2023	10
Final prep	9/20/2023	7	9/29/2023	9
Event day	10/1/2023	1	10/2/2023	1

Within the start date column, highlight all the dates, and then on your keyboard, press the shortcut key control together with one (CTRL + 1). That opens up the format cells dialogue, and it's currently set to the date format.

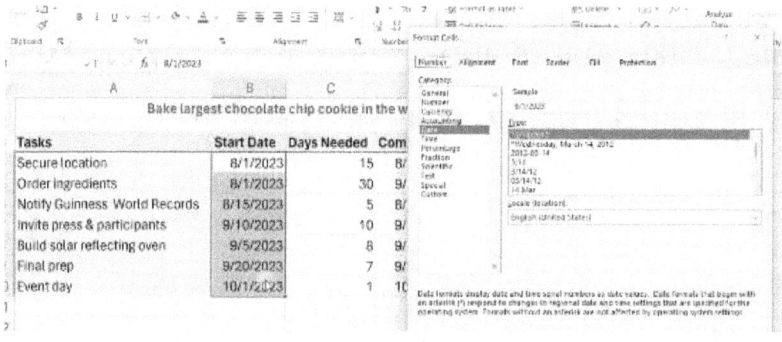

Click on General on the top and then click on OK. You are ready to insert a Gantt chart but don't need all the data. Highlight all the tasks, highlight the start date, press the control key on your keyboard, and highlight the adjusted length. With all the data selected, click on

Insert at the top tabs. Go to the insert options and click on recommended charts.

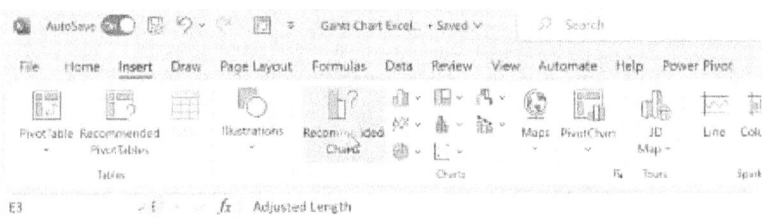

That opens up the insert chart dialogue, and you have some recommended charts. Click on all charts, and you have all the different types of charts. Assuming you want to use a bar chart, click on it. Select the bar option, click the second option for a stacked bar, and click OK. It has now inserted a chart.

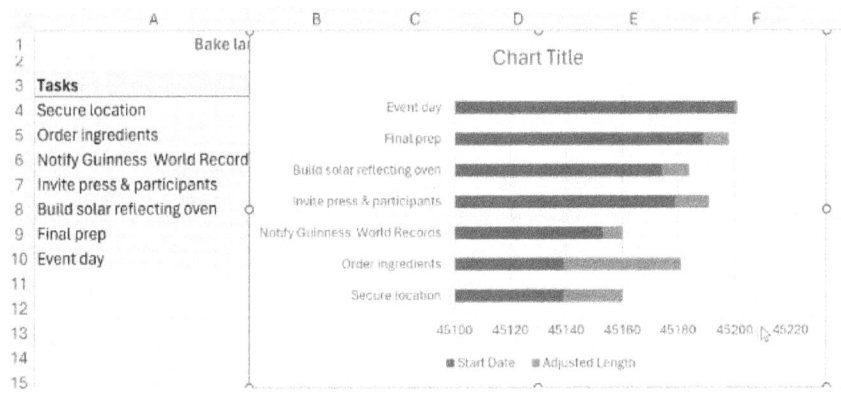

You'll notice that the dates show up as numbers, but you can change it back as a date. Again, highlight all date cells, press control + 1 on the keyboard (ctrl +1), click a date on the format cell, change that back to a date type, and click ok.

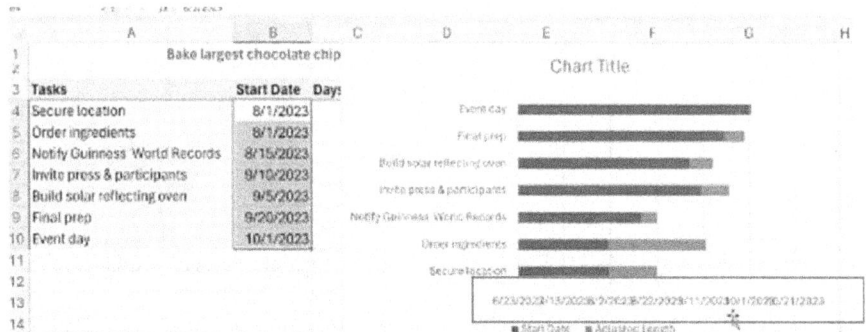

The chat doesn't yet look like a Gantt chart. So, to change that, double-click on the blue series, opening up a panel to format the data series. Over on the left-hand side, click on the paint bucket.

Select no fill and click on no line below. Then, close out to look a bit more like a Gantt chart.

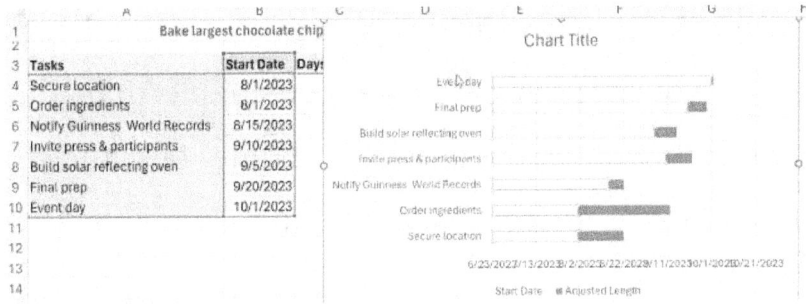

When you look at the task list, notice they're not in the same order. On the chat, there is an event day at the top, but over the table, it's at the very bottom. So, you need to reverse the order, so they both align. Double-click on the task list, and it opens up the pane again on the right-hand side called the format axis. Make sure you're in the axis options, and within axis options, scroll down just a bit, and you'll notice a checkbox next to categories in reverse order. Check that box, and you'll see they're the same.

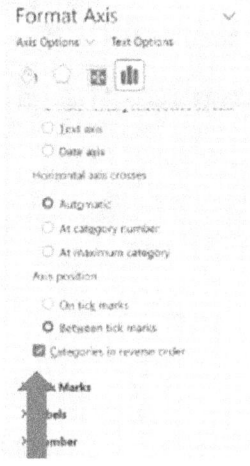

Next, on the top, if your dates run into each adjacent date and you need it to be more readable than that. Click on the dates, go to the home tab and the alignment category, and click on that to angle the text.

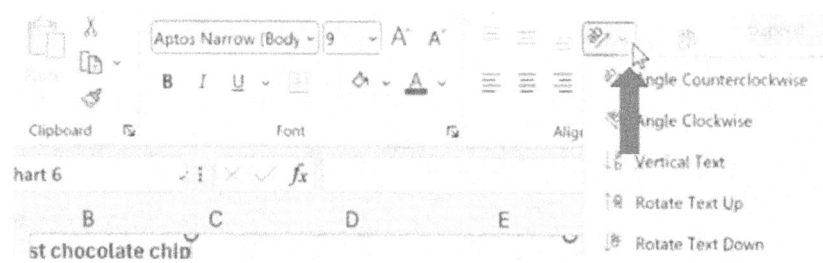

You'll notice a large gap in this Gantt chart before the first task starts. Double-click the dates above and over the right-hand side in the format axis pane, and ensure you're in the axis options category. There, you can set the bounds. Highlight the number in minimum, and if the first task doesn't start until 8/1, type in 8/1/2023 and hit enter, which removes the gap.

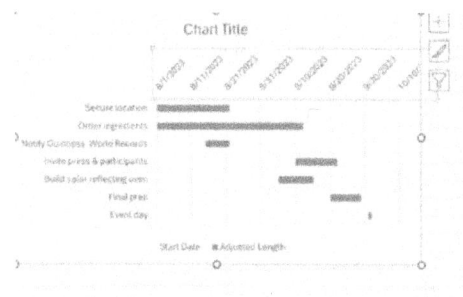

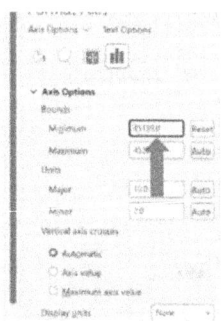

You can also do the same for the end date or the maximum. Highlight the value and type in 10/2/2023. Then hit enter, and you'll notice that the Gantt chart fits directly within the space.

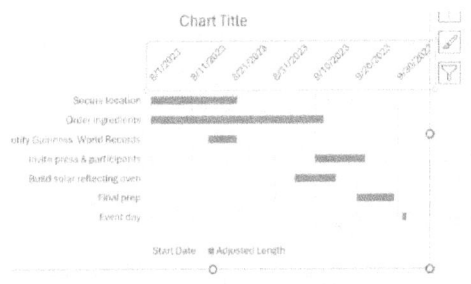 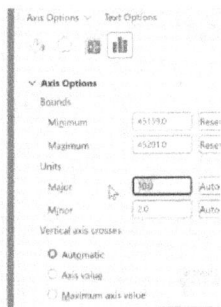

You can make a few more tweaks to enhance its appearance. They are all 10 days in the major lines, but let's say you want it to track each week. Go over to the right-hand side. Instead of having a 10 in the major, type in a 7 and then hit enter, which tracks each week.

You can also remove the legend at the bottom of the chart. Select the legend and then click on delete. As a final touch, you can update the chart title. Click on the chart title, and in the formula bar, make the title dynamic by entering the equals sign. That lets Excel know that you are about to enter a formula, and then select the cell with the title and hit enter, incorporating the title directly into the chart.

Another thing is, let's say you updated the title in the table. Instead of the initial title, you suggested the updated one. Hit enter, and you'll see that the chart or the Gantt chart automatically updates. You now have a beautiful Gantt chart and could do that simply by inserting a stacked bar chart and then hiding a portion of the bar chart. Even though Excel has no option for a Gantt chart, you could still make one. Sometimes, you just have to be creative.

Tasks	Start Date	Days Nee
Secure location	8/1/2023	
Order ingredients	8/1/2023	
Notify Guinness World Records	8/15/2023	
Invite press & participants	9/10/2023	
Build solar reflecting oven	9/5/2023	
Final prep	9/20/2023	
Event day	10/1/2023	

Bake biggest chocolate chip cookie in the world